# OPTIONS STRATEGIES FOR MONTHLY INCOME

## DAVID J. MELILLI

# CONTENTS

# DEDICATION

*First and foremost, without him taking my hand and walking me to shore through the storm I would have died in that boat several times over. This is your Glory.*

*To Valerie thank you for bringing him*

*...my love.*

*To my son David Xavier – this is all for you son – everything is all for you.*

*To my mom who just loved and supported my dreams. Mom you were there every single time I was in need...every time...I love you.*

*To my dad who gave me the two things I needed to do everything I did... dad you know what they were. I love you.*

*To Maggie and Josh – we have always been a team and always will be.*

*To UB – still may take you up on that soda.*

*To David Vitarelli...we made it buddy – EFS to IFS to the fax cover sheet with the bald eagle...we made it.*

*To all of my clients...each one of you allow me to live my dream and do what I love and for that I will always be in your corner.*

*To Michael Schoor – my mentor – to the man who taught me in a short amount of time this business – to the man that always gave me the advice he knew I needed – who stopped what he was doing to help me – to one of the greatest. Thank you.*

*To the eleven critical individuals that helped me get here – if you're one of them you know it. Thank you.*

*And to my readers, I suspect you are reading it because buying options is a zero sum (often negative game)*

*Email me at davidm@capstonesuccess.com with questions and for the best time for us to chat.*

## DISCLAIMER

This document is geared towards providing exact and reliable information in regards to the topic and issue covered. The publication is sold with the idea that the publisher is not required to render accounting, officially permitted, or otherwise, qualified services. If advice is necessary, legal or professional, a practiced individual in the profession should be ordered.

From a Declaration of Principles which was accepted and approved equally by a Committee of the American Bar Association and a Committee of Publishers and Associations.

The information provided herein is stated to be truthful and consistent, in that any liability, in terms of inattention or otherwise, by any usage or abuse of any policies, processes, or directions contained within is the solitary and utter responsibility of the recipient reader. Under no circumstances will any legal responsibility or blame be held against the publisher for any reparation, damages, or monetary loss due to the information herein, either directly or indirectly.

The information herein is offered for informational purposes solely, and is universal as so. The presentation of the information is without contract or any type of guarantee assurance.

# PRELUDE

Greed is good. At least that's what Michael Douglas told us in the movie, *Wall Street*.

At first glance, it seems that a lot of people must have the stock market all figured out. After all, if you watch any news channel on the financial markets, you'll see plenty of people dressed in smart suits, crisp white shirts, and fashionable ties. Most of them attended prestigious universities, such as Harvard, Wharton, or Stanford, to name a few. They speak with confidence about what the stock market has done in the past, is doing now, and will do in the future. All of these self-proclaimed "gurus" use the prestige of their academic degree to make predictions regarding the financial market.

Veteran traders and portfolio managers realize and accept the reality that that the stock market is unpredictable. No one can predict its behavior with 100% accuracy; even 50% accuracy has been impossible to achieve.

While we cannot predict the future despite what the investment professionals, research analysts and seasoned economists suggest on a daily basis. With that being said, there are a variety of trading strategies that we can utilize to maximize our probability of making profit, minimize our probability of a loss, or even to form some combination between the two.

## US STOCK MARKET BACKGROUND

The US stock market is comprised of many of the finest companies in the United States. The Dow Jones Industrial Average is comprised of 30 of the largest companies in the United States. This is represented to the public as a "basket" of stocks that are weighted together, meaning that each stock makes up a percentage of the index causing an average value. Together, the stocks in the Dow Jones are worth almost 7 trillion dollars.

The New York Stock Exchange, located at 11 Wall St in New York City, is the largest stock exchange in the world based on the total market cap of the securities listed on the exchange. Many of the oldest publicly traded companies are listed on the NYSE, and it is an extremely important market for the entire world. The Nasdaq Exchange at One Liberty Plaza in New York is the second-largest exchange in the world by market cap. An important difference between the Nasdaq and the NYSE is that the Nasdaq was the world's first electronic exchange (no open-outcry pits). This technological difference is fitting for the Nasdaq, as most of the world's tech giants (Amazon, Facebook, etc.) are listed on the Nasdaq exchange.

Just as the New York Stock Exchange is real, so is the cash we exchange in the stock market when we are selling options. As is so often the case when we work with electronic representations on our computers, it becomes easy to forget that we are working with real money. If we gain ten dollars, we have ten actual dollars of unrealized gains above our initial investment. When we lose ten dollars, we are ten actual dollars below our initial portfolio value. Our natural response when facing these situations is to do what will make us feel better in that moment; sell low then buy high. This phenomenon supports my theory as to why it is particularly important to have strong mental discipline, along with guidelines and trading rules that we adhere to. It is far better to be prepared for multiple disaster scenarios than to be caught by surprise.

Many firms have 'blown up' because they were caught by surprise and on the wrong side of a bad trade.

Those of us who've worked in the investment space for many years, nevertheless, find ourselves stopped in our tracks and wondering exactly what the heck just happened as we watch the market turn against us. After all, we knew what the market was going to do, how it was going to move, and we made our trade according to that knowledge. Often, this knowledge comes from years of experience, along with information that we've collected from co-workers, industry trade sources such as newspapers and websites, and those glorious sudden flashes of intuition that come when we least expect it.

If you are going to participate in the stock market in any capacity, you must understand an important truth about the financial marketplace. You need to recognize and understand that there is no amount of preparation, practice, or mathematical ability that will make sure you always make a good trade. The stock market involves many variables that you can't control. There is inherently some randomness that may cause a trade to be unprofitable. In his book, Fooled By Randomness, legendary derivatives trader Nassim Taleb elegantly proved that luck plays a very important and strong role in whether a trader is extremely profitable or un-profitable. By reading this book, I hope that you can learn from my experiences while skipping the trials and errors of mistakes I've made. I believe it was Freud who said, "Seek pleasure and avoid pain." Nothing is more pleasurable than a a successful trade, conversely closing a trade with a loss can derail your future success. .

## LET'S MAKE YOU A WINNER.

In this book, my goal is to challenge your feelings that ultimately drive poor decisions that are aimed to relieve your fear and greed emotions. This is achieved with two-steps. First, and throughout the book, I'll address the mental attitudes that need to be put in place to be successful in the stock market regarding selling option contracts. Those mental attitudes can't be digressed without causing a significant amount of disorder, chaos, and entropy in all of your other choices.

As you'll read, if your mental attitude and decision-making process is abandoned, you'll find yourself flailing about, adrift and without direction, like a sailor in a rowboat with only one oar.

We will walk through specific examples and strategies that will increase your success when selling options. This book is designed to be read thoroughly and referenced repeatedly as you try various methods of selling options. Just as each of us looks at a dinner menu and chooses what suits our palate, certain aspects of selling options will appeal to you while others will appeal to someone else. Thus, I'm providing a number of ways to sell options.

# CHAPTER ONE

## The Financial Crisis

*"An investment in knowledge pays the best interest."*
*- Benjamin Franklin*

The 2008 Financial Crisis is one of the most significant events in US history. In the months leading up to and following the crash, the housing market suddenly stopped being a way to make easy money in unsustainable amounts – causing the global economy to collapse. This was largely due Wall Street's creation of complicated financial instruments on the housing market called Collateralized Mortgage Obligations (CMO) and derivative products known as Collateralized Debt Obligations or (CDO).

CDOs allow hundreds of investors to get paid on a single home mortgage for as long as the homeowner made the monthly payment; however, if that homeowner could no longer afford the monthly payment, it wasn't just a single investor that realized a loss, it was hundreds of them. When an insurance company insures a home in the event of a fire, it is required to pay the homeowner if the house burns down, right? Well, insurance companies were selling fire insurance policies for a single property to more than one person. This created a situation where, if that house caught fire and burned down the insurance company may be required to pay one hundred people or maybe a thousand people the same amount that they paid to the actual homeowner. On Wall Street, we call this leverage.

By some measures, leverage in the five major investment banks was around 40:1; meaning a single dollar loss would create a forty dollar loss. As a final touch, you might want to add some regulatory negligence tied to the rating agencies in charge of defining the risk on most if not all housing investment products. This created a massive bubble on the $32-trillion-dollar housing market. That's approximately the same size as all the publicly traded companies combined (Russell 3000 index covers 98.5% of USA's market capitalization). It wasn't healthy economic growth, and what followed was arguably the worst financial crisis in history.

In January 2008, the Federal Reserve started to notice an unusual increase in foreclosures. This was caused by a system where the original lender was not concerned about the ability of the borrower to repay the loan as it was immediately selling the loan to Wall Street. The investment banks then "pooled" all of the loans together and sold them to investors all over the world. This relieved them of the borrowers' ability to repay the loan as well. At that time, the major investment banks carried leveraged sub prime mortgages on their balance sheets in massive amounts and keep this relatively secret.

In February 2008, foreclosures were not going down; in fact, they were moved up to sixty percent, three points higher than January's print of fifty-seven percent. Interest rate drops in January were quickly digested by the markets. Despite warnings from several of the most seasoned economists, most professionals rejected the idea that the whole US housing market was in a massive price bubble. The impending doom was even dismissed by several of the leading US government officials and economic advisers, including Ben Bernanke.

## JULY 2005 INTERVIEW WITH BEN BERNANKE:

*INTERVIEWER:* Tell me, what is the worst-case scenario? Sir, we have so many economists coming on our air and saying, "Oh, this is a bubble, and it's going to burst, and this is going to be a real issue for the economy." Some say it could even cause a recession at some point. What is the worst-case scenario, if in fact we were to see prices come down substantially across the country?

**BERNANKE:** Well, I guess I don't buy your premise. It's a pretty unlikely possibility. We've never had a decline in house prices on a nationwide basis. So, what I think is more likely is that house prices will slow, maybe stabilize: might slow consumption spending a bit. I don't think it's going to drive the economy too far from its full employment path, though.

Bernanke attended Harvard University in 1971, where he graduated with an A.B. degree, and later with an A.M. in economics summa cum laude in 1975. He received a Ph.D. degree in economics from the Massachusetts Institute of Technology in 1979 after completing and defending his dissertation, Long-Term Commitments, Dynamic Optimization, and the Business Cycle. Bernanke's thesis argued that businesses confronted by uncertainty are inclined to scale down on capital expenditure, investment outlay and recruitment until favorable information is obtained. Bernanke had an intimate understanding of the Great Depression and understood the importance of investor confidence. In Bernanke's view, the trigger of the Great Depression was a weakening of America's banking system by worried depositors who withdrew their money, which caused a severe panic and the failure of numerous banks. It was more the instability of financial institutions than the reduction in-the-money supply that toppled the U.S. economically and kept the stock market from regaining its 1929 highs until the 1950s.

> *"Importantly, in the 1930s, in the Great Depression, the Federal Reserve, despite its mandate, was quite passive and, as a result, the financial crisis became very severe, lasting essentially from 1929 to 1933."* —Ben Bernanke

In 2008, Ben Bernanke had accepted the very premise he rejected in 2005 and started to intervene more aggressively by lowering interest rates from 5.25% to 0.00% as he desperately tried to maintain investor confidence.

Trying to avoid the bankruptcy of the world's fifth largest investment bank and reassure worried investors, on March 17, 2008, The Federal Reserve guaranteed Bear Stearns' bad loans to facilitate the firm's acquisition by JP Morgan Chase.. Bernanke's decision can be easily understood with the following fact; Bear Stearns' stock went from $159 dollars a share to $2 dollars a share in 365 days.

During the following months The Federal Reserve's actions were highly debated and criticized. Then September 2008 arrived.

On Sept. 15, 2008, Lehman Brothers filed for bankruptcy with $639 billion in total assets and $619 billion in debt. Lehman's bankruptcy filing was the largest in history, as its assets far surpassed those of previous bankrupt giants, such as WorldCom and Enron.

After the Bear Stearns bailout, the Fed decided not to bailout Lehman, which triggered financial Armageddon. What it failed to realize was Lehman's brand value and its failures' effect on investors' confidence. It was a legendary investment bank and its decision to file bankruptcy sent shock waves across the worlds financial system.

That same day Bank of America acquired/saved Merrill Lynch. The following day, the Fed injected eighty billion dollars into AIG, the world's largest insurance company. On September 17th, Goldman Sachs and Morgan Stanley converted themselves from investment banks to bank holding companies to increase their protection by the Federal Reserve and gain access to much-needed bailout funds. Two days later, the Reserve Primary Fund "broke the buck" as a result of massive withdrawals from money market accounts.

On September 29, 2008, the House of Representatives rejected the Emergency Economic Stabilization Act of 2008, instituting the $700 billion Troubled Asset Relief Program. In response, the Dow Jones dropped 770 points, its largest single-day decline. A few days later, a second vote was taken, and Congress passed the Emergency Economic Stabilization Act of 2008.

In November 2008, GM, Ford, and Chrysler all asked to be saved as they relied on "short-term funding" from Wall Street to make payroll. Ford eventually didn't need it, but it was expected to affect one million jobs if the Fed didn't provide a back stop for all of the auto giants in addition to other industries being affected by the freeze in overnight lending.

Finally, on December 16, 2008, the federal funds rate was lowered to zero percent.

The central banks of the EU, Canada, Switzerland, Sweden, Japan, and China started a global coordination with the Fed, all lowering interest rates to nearly zero percent.

December 2008 was going to be the start of a new zero-interest rate era. This era would be defined by an economic strategy known as "quantitative easing" that would be implemented on a global scale. As markets were not inflationary, the plan could actually work. However, this has never been tested in history, especially on this scale. Bernanke was quoted on 60 Minutes, saying, "quantitative easing works in practice, not in theory."

After exactly ten years, in December 2019, the Fed's benchmark interest rates were still much lower than the 5.25% rate of 2007 (hovering around 2.25%). The stock markets around the world had recovered from the crisis many times over. Although the global economy seems healthier now, there are indications that we may have storm clouds on the horizon, such as inverted yield curve, lack of inflation, and political uncertainty.

Think about the S&P 500 in general and how it was affected by the "Great Recession." On March 9, 2009, the S&P hit an all-time low of 666 during the trading day, finally closing at 676. That day in history, which is now referred to as "the day stocks bottomed out," was the rock-bottom point of a period that wiped away trillions of dollars' worth of assets.

Ironically, then-President Barack Obama essentially pinpointed the moment when stocks would bottom out. During a press conference on March 3, President Obama stated that "what you're now seeing is earning and profit ratios starting to get to the point where buying stocks is a potentially good deal if you've got a long-term perspective on it."

That "long-term perspective" presents a vital lesson that all investors must learn when it comes to the rise and fall of the S&P 500 and the management of their investment portfolios. The S&P 500 eventually stabilized and began moving higher. What changed from March 9 to March 10? The answer is simple, "nothing." If we take a deeper look – on March 9, two people went to the market; one of them entered a buy order and the other a sell order.

Which one would you have been? Which one made the correct decision? Obviously, the buyer. I know you are saying, "yes anyone can see that in hindsight" however, I, as well as other investors, were seeing an opportunity that came directly from their simple, but at times complex, preparation for that exact moment. This is an extreme example because calling the bottom is luck – however, investors who were buying all the stocks that were being sold during the market crash had two things that the sellers did not have. They did their homework and applied common sense to the situation, and they trained their mind to stay in complete control of their emotions.

**Some simple but deep questions to think about are:**

*Didn't the S&P 500 hit its highest level it will ever hit?*

*Can the S&P500 go to 0?*

*Who do you want to be on March 9th: the buyer or the seller?*

*If you do ten mock trades and allow your emotions to make your decisions what was the outcome?*

*Now do ten mocks*

A report published by CNN in March 2015 stated that if you invested $100 into a fund that tracked the S&P 500 during that March 3, 2009, press conference, it would have experienced a 200% rate of return in the following 6 years.

Hopefully, these real-life examples of the ups and downs of the S&P 500 paint a picture for you that illustrates the significance of mental preparation. Only a few prepared minds forecasted the events that took place during the 2008 crisis. It took a toll on so many unprepared individuals, families, and companies. If you want to succeed in this industry, you have to be prepared.

***The Key Is To:***
*Prepare your mind*
*Manage your emotions*
*Make wise decisions that will not sabotage your long-term endeavors.*

*Stay disciplined to your strategy – epically when you are on the selling side – if you buy back you will be buying when Implied Volatility is surging (fancy way of saying every idiot out there is just blindly buying – THIS IS WHEN WE WANT TO BE SELLING – and if we sold…go take a 30 min walk.*

*If you buy high – you buy low selling low…Period*

*You are mad you sold out of your position last time and you won't allow it to happen to you again you will automatically lose your money*

*Options have two sides buyers and sellers – it's common to refer to one of them as the Casino and the other the Gambler…*

*Understand investing and making money in the market consistently is nearly impossible*

# CHAPTER TWO

## Train, Prepare, Focus, Repeat

*I want to start this chapter with something massive to get my point across. Unlike the Navy SEALs we will not be in danger nor will we have to do the physical training they do; with that being said I thought to myself if mental preparation, planning, practicing, and staying focused is the key to being successful who better to turn to then the greatest warriors on earth. Navy SEALs*

*For the context of this book we clearly are not referring to the life and death situation's these American Hero's put themselves through. We are also not referring to what you need to do mentally to what these warriors put themselves through physically.*

Interesting Fact: Navy SEALs shoot more bullets in training then the rest of our Armed Forces combined. Let that resonate for a few.

I believe that any investor who wants to be successful needs to train themselves mentally like a Navy SEAL. The premise behind this belief is the fact that Navy SEALs training is the toughest most demanding program on Earth. The goal of this training is not just to get the candidate into shape (because they usually already are) but to enable them to go beyond their limits or what they perceive as their limits. In this book we are going to focus on the mental aspect of a SEALs training.

The primary objective of this training is to prepare the Navy SEALS to face the worst possible situation in the best possible way. They need to learn how to focus, to make the right choices and to realize and understand what they're getting themselves into. When they do that, they become confident in their decisions, and that is exactly the kind of confidence an investor needs to develop.

SEALs are trained to face extreme challenges - both physical and mental, because of their sacrifices you only need to train your mind and the only way they can succeed is by living up to those challenges and by demonstrating determination, skills, and confidence. If an investor can train themselves to think, feel and act the same way as a SEAL, there is nothing that can stop them from making the right investments decisions.

Let's talk about the Navy SEALs Hell Week for a moment. This typically occurs during the third week of the first phase of the Navy SEALs' training program. During this Hell Week, the Navy SEAL has to undergo 7 days of cold and wet operational training that is extremely brutal, and that is normally done with less than four hours of sleep.

Why do you think they are made to endure this Hell Week? It is to test whether the SEAL in question has the mental aptitude, the physical endurance, the tolerance for pain and cold and the ability to survive in highly physical and mentally stressful situations. Every Navy SEAL has to demonstrate the right attitude and has to be a team player.

You need to understand that surviving this kind of training is not everyone's cup of tea. That is probably why only about 25 percent of SEAL candidates make it through this brutal Hell Week. It is considered to be the toughest training protocol in the US Military, but once a SEAL makes it through Hell Week, you better believe it that in their minds, they developed the confidence that they can do anything and that they can surpass any obstacle or hurdle that comes their way. For a Navy SEAL to be a Navy SEAL they have to train themselves to never quit simply because if they quit, they let their team down and that is not an option. You are not going to die or let your team member down; you are going to put your financial future at risk…

Many skills that are used by the Navy SEALs are applicable to investors. These include risk management, risk mitigation, projecting and forecasting, decision making, accountability, patience, and discipline to name a few.

If you, an investor, train yourself like a Navy SEAL, you are likely to perform like one. If you train your mind and emotions like a Navy SEAL trains his mind and emotions, you will realize that you are so well-prepared that nothing would ever scare you. Ever. You will perform better; you will have more confidence in your decisions; you won't be scared, and you will know that you've put your energy into something worthwhile and that and you've done it right. With that said, an amazing side effect of all this training your mind stuff will come a cool little thing – the confidence to do nothing and wait, be patient, you will gain the confidence to not engage in a specific investment.

You must be wondering how all this talk about Navy SEALs and how they train and how they undergo a brutal regime day-in-day-out is applicable to you. You're an investor. You haven't signed up for a rescue operation. You're not required to go rescue hostages captured by a mad terrorist. You're right. You don't. However, what you do need is to develop the mental strength that Navy SEALs develop after this rigorous training program.

SEALs spend a significant amount of time prepping because they know that being prepared is the key to success. You need to learn to do the same.

As an investor, you need to prepare. You need to know your market. You need to know the sector. You need to understand the company. You need to understand the competitors. You need to understand how the stock performs and why it performs the way it does. Don't limit yourself to understanding how much money you're going to make from an investment. Try to understand what you're investing in. The more prepared you are about what you've invested in, the better your decision-making power will be. This preparation will also be useful if you have to determine whether you need to sell or not.

As an investor, it's your job to figure out if something is a sound investment, however it's also your job to figure out that when it inevitably goes down in value to understand the reason and whether that reason is legitimate and company specific or not. As an investor, you should be aware that markets go up and down. There is always a risk, it is your job to handle that risk without succumbing to fear. People who succumb to fear when markets go down usually start selling. They start selling because they're scared. They are terrified because they're unprepared. They did not train themselves properly prior to putting their money at risk. Did you know that 88% of people lose money in great investments because they allowed fear to engulf them? They absolutely unequivocally did not have the mental strength you need to be successful in the investment business. I am going to teach you how to avoid this type of catastrophe.

When you train your mind and prepare yourself properly, you will be able to distinguish between a real situation and an imaginary situation. Just because a political situation goes volatile does not mean that you have to start selling. Think for a moment. Breath and concentrate. Remember the effort that you've put in. The time you've put in understanding the market, the sector, the company, and the competitors. There is no need to panic. Ask yourself if this is a real situation: is it company specific or simply based on factors that will potentially have no impact on my investment in the long run. If you are well-prepared, believe me when I say that your doubts and fears will disappear, and you will not panic when the market gets volatile.

There's yet another important Navy SEAL saying that we could all apply in our lives: "Get comfortable being uncomfortable." there is no doubt that for investors, researching, preparing and finding the right investment can be mentally draining and when you reach that point the value of the information you will need to depend on will not hold as much weight in the heat of the moment. With that said, most of the time, it will be quite uncomfortable. Will it work? Is this the right decision? Is this the right time to invest? There are so many fears and so many doubts when you are planning to make an investment. If you think like a Navy SEAL, you will train yourself to breach that fear. Just like a Navy SEAL spends weeks practicing clearing one four-bedroom structure, you as an investor should also learn to operate in situations that can be very uncomfortable. When you learn to do that, you will develop the ability to immunize yourself from these situations and to overcome any fears and any obstacles that might come your way.

Did you know SEAL Team Six spent six months rehearsing how to breach "his" compound – they were so prepared they had a complete plan to still execute the mission if one of the helicopters crashed.

These are the most extreme examples I can give and although money is the most fluid commodity, doing the wrong thing has ruined lives and will in the future. All you need to do is train your mind so that you can recognize a real threat or an imagined threat and that's done through research. All the time you spent preparing will help you remember the facts and make an educated decision rather than panic and lose your money. Remember how Navy SEALs train. They force themselves to do certain things that no one else would want to do, an 99% of us can't do and they go through it all because they first and foremost they are absolute hero's and the most deadly and feared group of warriors on Earth…by a wide margin. It's not called Hell Week for nothing. Hell, Week prepares them and helps them develop the skills and the mental strength they will need when they are actually in real hell.

As an investor our physical lives are not in danger nor do we do anything close to The SEALs Teams, however what we can learn from them is to "train, practice, train, practice, over and over again so their most dangerous and deadly missions become a work of art. Every single SEAL does exactly what they need to do and when they do it, it's done with precision. You want to make sure that the preparation you do before you buy anything is thorough, precise, accurate, and most importantly what you will turn too when things go down. I have GREAT news, when you are finally done you will not have to go on the most dangerous missions on earth today. Before you put your money in anything, you need to be confident, more confident then you've ever been about anything in life. If you're not, as soon as you start to lose money you're going to crumble like an eggshell because you're scared to death. You will start to question why you did this, and these thoughts and these doubts will outweigh a lot of flimsy thoughts that you put into your initial decision. In short, you really have to be confident in your decision. It is very scary to lose money, and I am quite sure you will lose money without any preparation or confidence.

Like I've mentioned before, investing can be a scary venture because you always have this feeling at the back of your mind that the market situation can suddenly change. It is this very feeling that you need to overcome, and you can do so the Navy SEALs way. Never let this feeling of the unknown interfere with your decision-making process. Never let it dictate or dominate your thoughts. If the SEALs let every nerve-wracking situation boggle their mind, they would fail at every mission. That is why they train, and they train incessantly. For an investor, this training includes research and research and more research.

*"Mastering others is strength.*
*Mastering yourself is true power."* – Lao Tzu

The simple two-word statement "Don't Panic" may seem easy to follow. However, when everything starts to fall apart, and your train of positive thoughts (or reasons you invested your money in that stock) are derailed or never existed in the first place, those two words of calmness and tranquility are usually the first two words to take a hike.

A study conducted at the California Institute of Technology suggested that successful traders often have high levels of emotional regulation, which helps them avoid the impulse to conform to the herd. In fact, one study showed even not having emotions at all might be helpful. In 2005, Carnegie Mellon, Stanford, and University of Iowa researchers looked at the investment behavior of a group of people with damage to the brain where emotions are concerned. Injuries left these people less capable of fear and some other emotions, but their basic intelligence remained intact. In a limited study, these participants with limited or lacking emotional capabilities in their brain performed better than their peers without the partial brain damage to the emotion regulation part in trading decisions. [1]

In one neuroeconomic research at the California Institute of Technology in 2014, Alec Smith, B. Douglas Bernheim, Colin F. Camerer, and Antonio Rangel found that successful traders indeed had different results from fMRI scans compared to their peers who couldn't manage to be as profitable. [2]

"The high-earning traders are the most interesting people to us," Camerer said in an interview. "Emotionally, they have to do something really hard."

Using fMRI data, researchers found that participants had increased activity in a specific brain region called the nucleus accumbent (NAcc) when they were told their trading results for the previous term. This was the same for all participants and wasn't surprising. However, one finding was very surprising to see. Less successful traders were very sensitive to NAcc activity. Following the activity, they bought a lot of risky assets. The traders with most success showed lower sensitivity to the same brain signal. It's not to say inactivity is the key to success; however, this is a great scientific finding in parallel of the importance of mastering the emotions and urges in investment decisions. Those emotions do not occur until you find yourself in the situation and that's why they are so difficult to prepare for beforehand. It takes a certain level of continuous mastery and preparation, as well as aftermath analysis.

Returning to the question of the high-earning traders, the researchers hypothesized that a part of the brain called the insular cortex might be the mastermind behind this. fMRI data shows that insula activity increased shortly before the traders switched from buying to selling. While others were following the herd instincts that conform to what everyone else is doing, they had the vision or emotional discipline to be able to see a different picture.

It is only natural to connect the decline of our emotions to the decline of our hopes and successes. For example, consider one of your favorite athletes at the end of a big game. As the highly anticipated victory slips through their fingers, it is not unlikely to see their emotional stability slip through the cracks as well.

You may see the athlete begin to cry on camera or display tell-tale signs of sadness/depression, even as they forcefully remind themselves still to smile for the camera and congratulate the winners. If they allow their emotions to take full control of the wheel, this might result in extremely negative publicity such as social media rants, unnecessary "soapbox" moments during post-event press conferences, and viral soundbites or memes will haunt them for years come into the picture.

The same type of emotionally impulsive reaction destroys the long-term potential of investments year after year. The nature of the S&P 500 is based on fluctuation: it is guaranteed that there will be highs and lows. It is impossible to guarantee that the S&P 500 will always increase or decrease, regardless of how much of a "sure thing" your investment option(s) may appear. Like a professional surfer, you must be mentally and emotionally prepared to ride the wave from top to bottom, patiently waiting for the next wave to come around.

Throwing in the towel too quickly, just because you are experiencing a "down moment", may cause you to miss out on a lot of prosperity in the future.

**ASK YOURSELF:**
*Who do you want to be:*
*The person who sells stock at a low point or buys it?*

Investments are naturally scary and can be slightly nerve-wrecking when you consider the amount of money and assets invested. However, you should never allow this state of the "unknown" to cause your emotions to dominate, dictate, or even interfere with your decision-making process. Even inexperienced investors will agree that it takes a lot of careful thought and research when making investment decisions. Making those types of decisions solely based on emotions may seem immature and unrealistic. However, when the stock market fluctuates and the S&P 500 drops, it is usually those same "immature" and "unrealistic" emotions that cause investors to make decisions that they would more than likely not have made if they had kept their emotions in check.

Covered calls and selling options can help with this. Researchers Nikunj Kapadia and Edward Szado, CFA from the University of Massachusetts, Amherst, showed in a very detailed 15-year-long study on covered calls that covered calls outperformed the underlying Russell 2000 index. [3] (8.87% versus 8.11%; at three-quarters of the risk with standard deviations: 16.57% versus 21.06%). This result was achieved despite market conditions that were unfavorable to these strategies, such as the period between March 2003 to October 2007.

*Note: Covered calls are known to perform optimally during flat or slightly bullish markets. We will talk about this very powerful tool in great detail in other chapters, but it is just one of the indications of how potent structured derivatives can be in the hands of wise investors.*

A vast number of investors are quick to sell when the market is at the bottom. Nevertheless, many of those same investors are quick to kick themselves when they realize that the apparently empty caves that they impulsively left behind when times were tough were actually gold mines. It's just a matter of determining whether or not you have the insight, patience, and self-control to wait it out and reap the rewards in the long run.

*"Greed is a bottomless pit which exhausts the person in an endless effort to satisfy the need without ever reaching satisfaction."* – Erich Fromm

One of the first finance tips that the average person learns is to avoid greed at all costs. Various religions teach about the poisonous danger of greed and the unhealthy love of money. As parents teach their children to appreciate the value of a dollar, they strive to engrave the message of not being greedy into their minds and hearts as well. There is an extensive list of inspirational quotes on the internet that also encourage the need to prohibit greed from taking over.

*"The highest wealth is the absence of greed." – Seneca*

Sadly, though, it is the detrimental danger of greed that compels numerous investors to buy into an investment prior to being fully prepared. As a result, they are not properly prepared mentally or emotionally for the losses that WILL arise. When you take the time to study investment options and stocks carefully to identify the specific roads to travel, you have the time to prepare yourself for the losses that may come along the way as well. It is similar to planning a road trip in advance – giving yourself plenty of time to analyze the weather forecasts and road conditions that you may face along the way. If you decide to take an unexpected detour based on emotional impulses and uneducated "gut feelings," though, then you may quickly find yourself on a dead-end street or at the top of the hill where the only direction left to go is down or wait a flat trend for years without any possible movement.

You will find very powerful tools in later chapters of this book explaining how to ride different waves with structured derivative products. The secrets of covered calls, iron condors and vertical spreads are only some of them. I tried to share my years of experience in the financial markets so that you can be aware of these initially complex looking financial tools that the super wealthy practice all the time. But they are not available to only the super wealthy, although they usually are the ones to discover them and benefit from them. You will also learn that these financial tools are not that complicated after all and there are simple ways to conquer and master these strategies.

There is usually a point in time when the question gets asked after an investment, "Was I right about this investment or was this not a good place to put my money?"

During a period of unexpected panic and emotional distress over declining stock performance, it is easy to forget that ETFs and indices are designed to rise. Still, an overwhelming sense of physical and mental discomfort settles in when people see the value of their money drop lower and lower. That is usually when doubts and uncertainties show their ugly heads, making the investors feel uncomfortable and reluctant about retaining those investments. They may even start to come up with a list of reasons why they should sell immediately without any further hesitation.

Studies have shown that the longer the market is down, the more people will sell their investments. Instead of realizing that these losses are temporary, people tend to sell when the market is low, and they are guaranteed to walk away with a loss.

In addition to keeping your emotions away from the steering wheel and avoiding any greedy tendencies, you must be able to prepare yourself mentally to take full advantage of this well-hidden opportunity. Mental preparation.

*"Be fearful when others are greedy and greedy when others are fearful." – Warren Buffet*

Instead of selling when you experience an overwhelming sense of panic, studies have shown those are the best times to buy! As mentioned earlier, like a patient surfer in the middle of the ocean, the bullish waves will return. If you are quit and swim back to shore, you will miss out on all of them. However, if you patiently "tread water" in the stock market while retaining your existing investments and exploring new opportunities, that approaching wave could very well end up taking you straight to the bank.

Remember what happened to the S&P in 2009 during the "Great Recession." However, think about where the S&P is now. It is designed to go low at times, but eventually it will bounce back. The timing of those comebacks may vary, but the overall resilient nature of the stock market remains intact. You must view the S&P as a marketplace just like anything else.

Within the standard marketplace, when prices drop on an in-demand item, most consumers are quick to purchase it. Why? It is simply because they rightfully believe that the price will eventually return to its original price (if not higher), based on consumer demand. Think about how crazy consumers go over Black Friday deals – especially when they are able to buy high-value products for a fraction of the price they would have paid otherwise.

The wise approach is to view the S&P the same way that a frugal consumer views Black Friday. As soon as those numbers go down, you should swoop in like a hawk – fully assured that the numbers will rise again but determined to take full advantage of the marketplace in the meantime.

Unless you think that the U.S. economy is going to fail, it's safe to assume that the S&P and other indices will succeed and rise as they are designed to do. It is just a matter of staying in control of how you react mentally, emotionally, and financially in the meantime.

## INTRODUCTION TO OPTIONS

Explain the basics of calls and puts here (call/put owner has the OPTION to purchase/sell the underlying asset at a specified price on a specified day, etc.)

Start with the explanation of LONG calls and LONG puts, as these are easier to understand. Most traders start with buying options because they are cheap and can make you a lot of money in a very short amount of time. In the previous chapters we discussed The Financial Crisis as well as the mental preparation of a Navy SEAL. You will need both chapters to be successful in generating income but not as much as you would if you were buying options

## Option Value at Expiration

▸ Call option: has positive value when the stock price is greater than the strike price

▸ Put option: has positive value when the stock price is less than the strike price.

▸ Value of call option <u>at expiration</u>:

$$C_T = Max(0, S_T - X)$$

▸ Value of put option <u>at expiration</u>:

$$P_T = Max(0, X - S_T)$$

▸ 8                                                                    FIN 404

A statistical fact: 75% of options expire worthless. Which mean 75% of people that buy the option you sell on day one for monthly income will take a 100% loss on day 30.

Something to keep in mind – most options traders buy into them in anticipation of a violent, quick move in the direction they want.

## Profit at Expiration

▶ Example: Consider the value at expiration to a call option and a put option on Microsoft stock, both of which have an exercise price of $50. Assume that the price of the call option was $6, and the price of the put option was $6 when purchased. (Ignore time value of money for the option premiums).

| $S_T$ | 35 | 40 | 45 | 50 | 55 | 60 | 65 |
|---|---|---|---|---|---|---|---|
| Long Call | -6 | -6 | -6 | -6 | -1 | 4 | 9 |
| Short Call | 6 | 6 | 6 | 6 | 1 | -4 | -9 |
| Long Put | 9 | 4 | -1 | -6 | -6 | -6 | -6 |
| Short Put | -9 | -4 | 1 | 6 | 6 | 6 | 6 |

▶ 12                                                                 FIN 404

## Profit at Expiration ($X$=\$50, $C$=\$6, $P$=\$6)

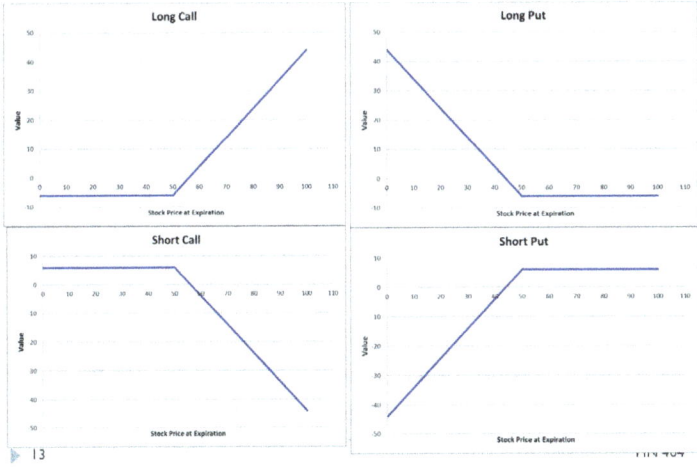

▶ 13                                                                 FIN 404

*There are two components of an option price: Intrinsic value & time value*

Unlike buying options, selling options puts you in an obligatory situation. With buy options, you pay a premium and you purchase an option or a right without the obligation. However, when you sell options, you get paid the premium for the obligation to sell your shares at the strike price at which you sold the call. Although it can be very profitable, this is the reason why selling options requires knowledge, discipline, and caution.

Now that you have some specific knowledge about option pricing and variables that affect the option price, let's take a look at two main components of an option's value. This part is much easier to understand, and it is also more crucial to know.

An option is a combination of two different values during its life. These are intrinsic value and time value. At the end of an option's life or (at expiration), time value is equal to zero. Time value decreases in value as time passes and the option gets closer to its maturity or expiration date. Intrinsic value only changes as the underlying value changes. Let's look closely:

Intrinsic value: *This is simply the price difference between the strike price and underlying price.*

As you probably know, a call option is in-the-money when stock price is above the strike price and put option is in-the-money when the stock price is below the strike price.

Let's take a look at four different scenarios, two for, each call and put:

**Scenario 1:**
A Call option on Apple (AAPL) with 90 days to maturity and $120 strike price. (Assume Apple is trading at $150 today)

The intrinsic value of this option is 150 − 120 = $30 (the option's actual value) and, further, it has a time value coming from 90 days to maturity that is calculated with more complex mathematical formulas. (More on time value in the upcoming chapters). Time value will decrease every day as time passes and it will be zero at the end of the term, such that the only remaining value of the option will be the intrinsic value. Verdict: In-the-money

**Scenario 2:**
Call option on AAPL with 90 days to maturity and $160 strike price. (Assume Apple is trading at $150 today)

The intrinsic value of this option is $150 - 160 = -10 = 0$. You wouldn't exercise your option to buy the stock at $160 while it's trading at $150 in the market, so the option contract is worthless. However, the option still has its time value left. As the time to maturity decreases (i.e. we get closer to expiration), the time value decreases to zero. Out-of-the-money options expire worthless 75% of the time, which is why it's vital to keep your composure when the stock you're selling against experiences some volatility.

Verdict: Out-of-the-money

**Scenario 3:**
Put option on AAPL with 90 days to maturity and $140 strike price. (Assume Apple is trading at $150 today)

The intrinsic value of this option is $140 - 150 = -10 = 0$. You wouldn't exercise your option to sell the stock at $140 while it's trading at $150, so this right amounts to zero value for you. But the option still has and only has its time value. If it expires like this, time value will also go to zero on maturity and option's total value will equal zero.

Verdict: Out-of-the-money

**Scenario 4:**
Put option on AAPL with 90 days to maturity and $160 strike price. (Assume Apple is trading at $150 today)

The intrinsic value of this option is $160 - 150 = 10$. Intrinsic value is $10. And the option still has its time value. If it expires like this, time value will also go to zero on maturity and option's total value will equal $10.00 dollars multiplied by 100 (equity contracts have a multiplier of 100). Verdict: In-the-money.

Now let's look at some of the dynamics of selling options.

## SELLING CALL OPTIONS

Both call options and put options have a time value and an intrinsic value. Thus, no matter what, as time passes, an option's time value will decrease. In addition to that, as time passes, the stock has to make larger moves to equal the option's prior value (for example, one week ago versus today).

When you sell or short a call option, you give your counterparty the right to purchase your stock at the strike price at a future date. So, if that asset, let's say Amazon, skyrockets until maturity, you have a huge debt of giving that stock to your counterparty at a much lower price. This is not a bad thing when we are using our assets to generate income on a monthly basis as we are more concerned about the income and not the stock price gains. Emotions will drive you to buy back the call at a higher price … when generating income, this is usually a huge mistake.

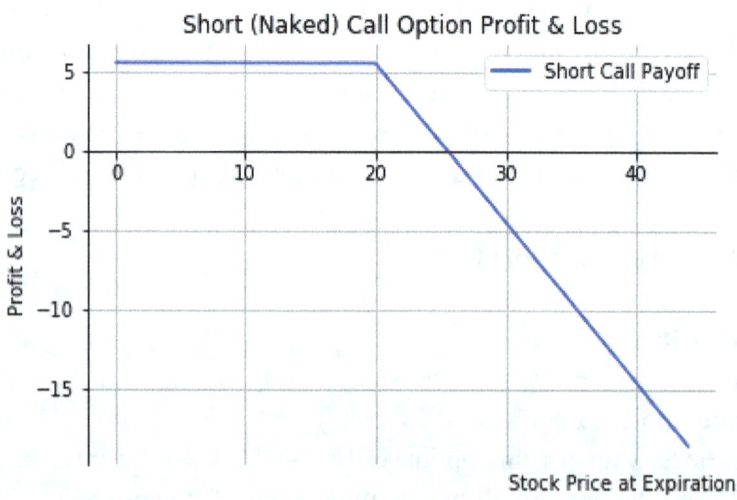

You are trading potential gains above the strike price you sold for guaranteed upfront income. Potential gains are the thing to remember.

## SELLING PUT OPTIONS

When you sell a put option, you sell your counterparty the right to sell an underlying at a predefined strike price. In other words, you promise to buy his/her stock at the strike price. So, if the underlying price keeps going down, you might lose a lot of money as you have agreed to buy it at a much higher price. This strategy is often used to buy back into a stock at the price you feel it's worth; you are sitting on cash earning the same (possibly more) monthly income to wait for the stock to come to you.

As the figure shows, selling naked put options is somewhat less risky than naked call options. Your potential gain is the premium you collected. But your potential losses are not infinite. The losses are limited to the underlying stock price (multiplied by 100). If your short put has a strike price of $30 and stock goes to zero, you are obliged to buy it at $30; although this loss of $3,000 is rather large, your risk is theoretically limited.

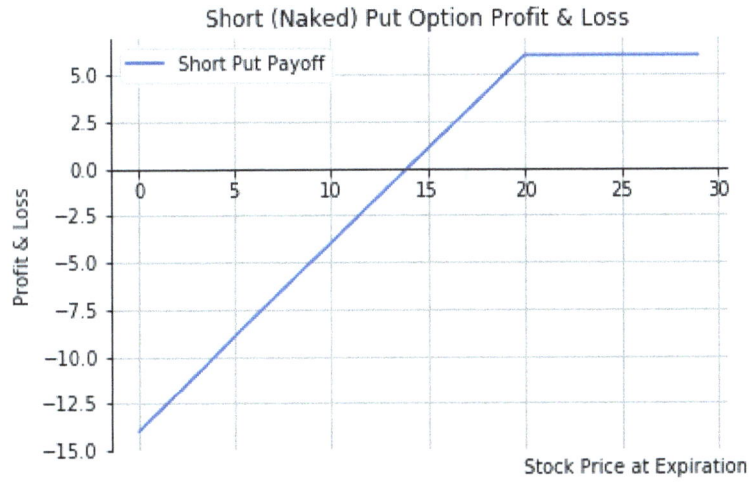

*Fun fact: Warren Buffett is notoriously known for selling put options.*

*Despite his views:*

*"I view derivatives as time bombs, both for the parties that deal in them and the economic system…"– 2002 Berkshire Hathaway Annual Report.*

Sometimes you have to follow what the man does and not what the man says.

In one famous case, Warren Buffett was interested in buying Coca-Cola stock. He felt the fundamental value was around $35 and, in April 1997, the stock was trading at $39. So, he sells 5 million put options at a strike price of $35. What happens here is he is happy to buy at $35 if the stock goes there. So, he writes himself a discount on the stock while collecting millions of dollars in premiums (approximately $7 million). This case shows that with the right knowledge and control over your naturally occurring emotions, you can be paid to have a discount on what you are interested in buying.

You might not be a hedge fund manager with massive capital under management, or an investment guru who can be so sure about valuation of a stock you can still implement this strategy with a little due diligence. You might not have the appetite to take increased risk or leverage your position. That's why it's important to understand option fundamentals explained in this book so far, and also the structured derivative strategies in the upcoming chapters will be very useful to tailor those strategies and outcomes using options.

You will see that by using options, you are not limited to only plain vanilla call and put options, but instead you can specifically design the strategies to your exact expectations by combining different option ingredients.

## Example 1: Naked call

Let's observe a short option strategy in more detail.

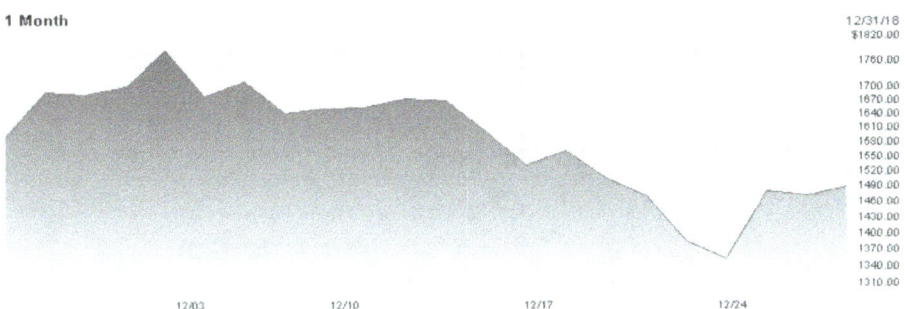

**Amazon Stock Chart for December 2018**

Below we see 2 call options on Amazon with strike prices of $1340 (on the left) and $1480 (on the right). Both had the same expiration date of December 28, 2018, and all charts show the data as of December.

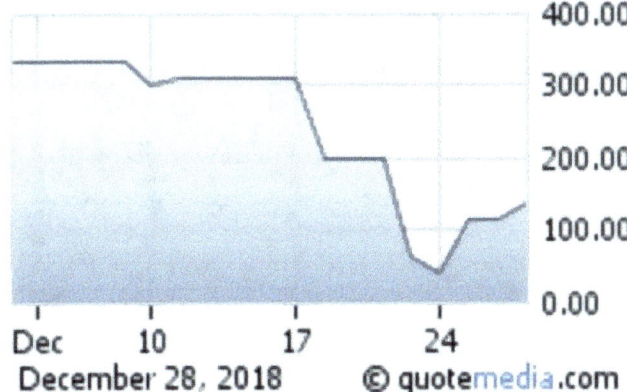

Type: Call, Underlying: Amazon (AMZN), Strike: $1340

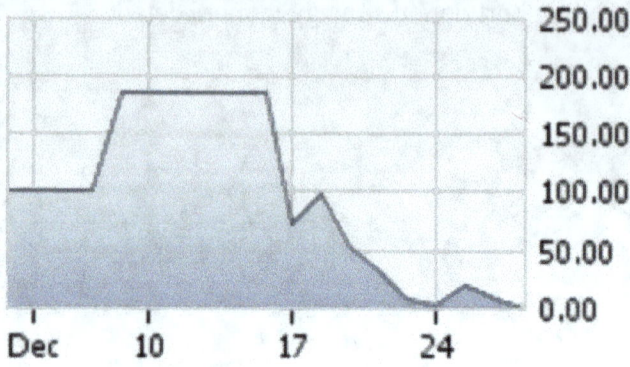

Type: Call, Underlying: Amazon (AMZN), Strike: $1480

**1st Option:**
You can see that 1st call with the strike of $1340 was deep in-the-money in the beginning of December. As AMZN shares start to decrease on the 17th through the 24th, this option decreases in value. On the 24th, the first option is nearly at-the-money and has very little intrinsic + time value is left. It shows approximately $1360 – $1340 = $20 intrinsic value. But from December 24th to 28th, as Amazon stock increases, the 1st option is in-the-money again and closes at expiration with an intrinsic value of approximately: $1470 - $1340 = $130.

**2nd Option:**
Again, this option starts declining in value as the stock price declines and on the 24th the option has almost zero value. This is because very little time value is left at this point (Only 4 days: 28th – 24th) and the option is out-of-the-money.

Short Call Perspective: If you shorted these call options, they would be in-the-money as the underlying price fell below the strike price. Let's say you sold the 1st option at around $325 (remember it is in-the-money by almost $300 at this point. So, if nothing changes, you still owe $300 to the buyer at the end of the term). As you are obliged to sell the counterparty a stock at $1340, as the stock price declines, your obligation becomes less costly.

On the 24th, as the option gets very close to the strike price, you almost realize all of your option premiums of $325 that you collected in the beginning. But, as the stock slightly increases again, the option expires in-the-money.

Let's say you end up replacing your stock obligation at $1465 and it costs you $125. You are still making a profit of $200. This is because you sold an expensive option (deep in-the-money) and it almost ended worthless. Another profit you have been realizing was time value. The option you sold has been losing its time value every day, which you collected up front (as part of the option price). We will look closer at the time value in the next chapter.

Regarding the 2nd option from a shorting perspective, it also has a similar profile (as the underlying price decreased over the contract time period). However, it expired worthless, since it was out-of-the-money at maturity and it wouldn't make sense for the option buyer to exercise it. So, you ended up realizing all of your profits from when you sold the option. Let's say you sold it at $100 and it expired at 0, the profit equals $100 in this case. (please ignore some of the discrete value jumps in the options' charts, these are likely caused by inactive periods and illiquidity)

## Example 2: Naked put
Now let's look at a put example on the same underlying stock.

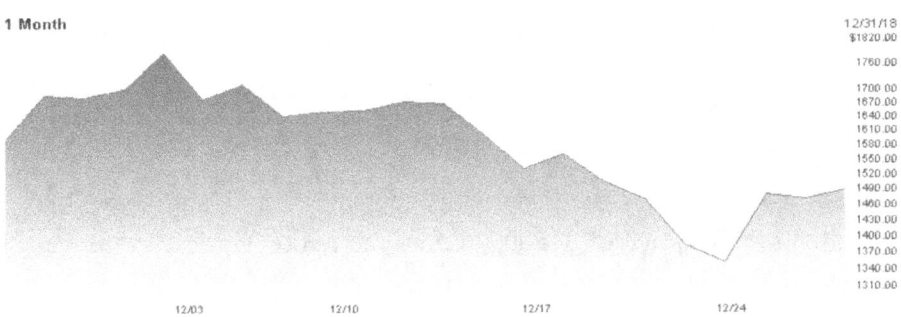

**Amazon Stock Chart for December 2018**

Below we see two put options on Amazon with strike prices $1500 (on the left) and $1360 (on the right). Both had the same expiration date of December 28, 2018, and all charts show the data for December.

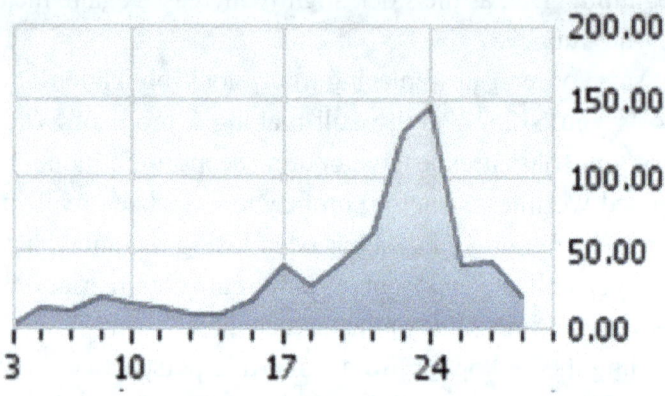

Type: Put, Underlying: Amazon (AMZN), Strike: $1500

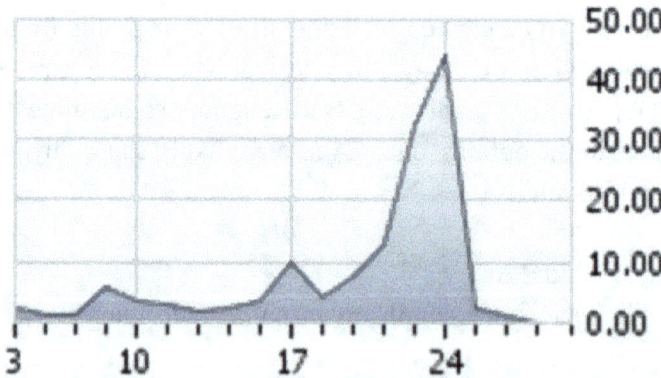

Type: Put, Underlying: Amazon (AMZN), Strike: $1360

**1st Option:**

Here we see that as the underlying fluctuates below and above the option's strike price of $1500, so does the option's price. In the beginning of December, as the stock is well above $1500, there is no intrinsic value and only some time value. It is interesting to see that this time value increases around the 10th of December, when the stock starts falling a bit.

This shows the dynamic nature of time value and how it's affected by several variables in a relatively complex manner. As we discussed, these variables include price difference, volatility, interest rate, and time left to maturity.

From December 17th to 24th, as the stock falls, the option sees a big rise in value. On the 24th, it reaches an intrinsic value of nearly $140 plus some time value, although time value is expected to be small at this point as it's so close to the maturity. (More on this in next chapter) The remainder of the period shows the volatile nature of option prices as the stock price starts increasing again, it almost becomes worthless again near the $1500 level. But, as it expires with stock price under the strike price, around $1480, the option manages to expire in-the-money with an intrinsic value of ~$20.

## 2nd Option:

This option also sees a wild ride during its life in December. Similar to the 1st option, we see no intrinsic value until around the 24th, when the underlying price falls below $1360. On the 24th, AMZN shares close at $1344 and the stock sees an intraday high and low of $1307 and $1396. We can see that this was reflected in the option price, as it trades at $40+. As soon as the shares start rising again and they pass $1360, the option rapidly goes to zero as both the intrinsic value and time value goes to zero.

Short Put Perspective: As you are selling puts, you are obliged to buy from your counterparty at the strike price. As the underlying decreases below strike price, you would have a loss in both instances around the 24th of December. This strategy is best used to pick your price for a particular stock – you would implement this strategy as a way to buy back into a stock at the price you want rather than the market price. Emotional Tip

**Option key points:**

1 – Option prices will go to zero if they expire out-of-the-money which happens approximately 75% of the time. This is fundamentally different than buying a stock or investing in an index. Options have no real value if the stock doesn't make and sustain an outsized move.

2 - Buying options carries no obligation but contains extreme risk. It gives you the right to a stock's dollar value above a certain price on a future date. Selling call options, however, will require you to sell your shares at a certain price; if you don't have shares to sell, you must buy them at the current market price and then deliver to the option holder.

3 - Options require a high amount of caution and sophistication. Option prices can move up and down violently, especially when the underlying is flirting with the strike price or the option contract is close to expiration. It can go to zero quickly, which it usually does at expiration. This is what we need to focus on because we have collected our monthly income on day one.

4 - Selling options is used to create defensive strategies in a portfolio, create monthly income, or to buy or sell a stock at a price you choose. Remember, options are inherently derivative products; there are so many ways to engineer the specific outcome you desire. Many funds are known to create delta-neutral, derivative strategies where they only look to profit from time decay or theta (time value) by shorting options.

*(If you are not very familiar with Greeks, don't worry; I will explain them further in a dedicated chapter.)*

5- By utilizing sophisticated strategies such as covered calls, iron condors, and PMCCs, you can profit in a market that is completely flat. A flat market will reduce the dollar value of the options we sell, however it's unlikely we will ever get assigned.

6- Option selling involves strategies that are both covered and uncovered (naked). They can have very different risk/return profiles. A "naked" or uncovered strategy means selling an option on an underlying security that you don't own. Naked positions in options can be an extremely risky investment strategy and should only be used when absolutely necessary. Some of the main uses of naked positions are hedging, leveraged speculation, decreasing capital requirements, etc.

7- As for all income generating strategies, any kind of trading knowledge, research, emotional preparation, experience, or skills make a huge difference. So, when selling options for income, covered or uncovered, remember they are very powerful tools if used properly. You need to understand the mechanics of how they work; accept that selling them is always putting.

# CHAPTER THREE

## Selling Option's Understanding The Basics

*The mechanics of all option strategies were designed to work out in the sellers favor 75-80 percent of the time. This is where your mental and emotional preparation need to step up to the plate.*

Ask any wise man and he will tell you that becoming professional is not something that happens overnight; it takes time and energy to get there. It usually equals sweat equity and, in this case, a lot of it. However, I wrote a book that will give you the knowledge and tools that you will need to sell options successfully on a consistent basis. Once you understand the dynamics and characteristics of options, the underlying advantages will prove to be very potent tools. The energy you put into this will save you lots of time and unnecessary losses that are usually involved during the learning curve of options.

### A BRIEF HISTORY

Although the history of derivatives can be traced back to the late 17th century when a Samurai in Japan traded rice for future items in demand at the time; options as we know in modern day, started much more recently.

In 1973, two academics with prestigious backgrounds progressively came up with an idea of what would become a historical breakthrough in option pricing. The formula inherits its name from these two men: Black and Scholes (Merton would be added later, with his dividend-effect contributing to the formula).

The formula that is used to price options is a complicated calculation that has several underlying variables. Black and Scholes used variables such as the market price of the stock,the option's strike price, both historical and implied volatility, time to expiration which is often referred to as time decay, and the risk-free interest rates in the market. These variables were used in several complex mathematical formulas; in addition to some normal distribution modeling and the result was the widely accepted pricing formula for stock options in today's market. Full technical details of the Black and Scholes Formula are beyond the scope of this book. However, I will share more technical details in the upcoming pages for those of us who love math.

Interestingly enough, Black and Scholes faced great difficulty having their paper published in the more prestigious journals available at the time. Initially, using differential equations and distribution models was unexpected and confusing. With slight intervening by Merton, their paper would finally be published, they were later awarded a Nobel prize for their contributions in field of economics in 1990.

I felt it was important to visit the history behind this Nobel Prize-winning formula. In today's world our computers handle most of the calculations required to price options in today's markets. Even at hedge funds with highly skilled traders, you will see simple Excel formulas, on spreadsheets being used, to calculate the option price.

In the upcoming chapters, we will look at examples that illustrate how the variables work in real life trades.

The Black and Scholes Formula multiplies the stock price by the cumulative standard normal probability distribution function (C is the Call Option pricing. P is the Put Option pricing).

It then takes the net present value (NPV) of the strike price (discounted using the continuously compounding risk-free rate, annualized), multiplied by the cumulative standard normal distribution which is then subtracted from the previous calculation.

$$C = S_0 N(d_1) - Ke^{-r_cT}N(d_2)$$
$$P = Ke^{-r_cT}N(-d_2) - S_0 N(-d_1)$$

$$d_1 = \frac{\ln\left(\frac{S_0}{K}\right) + \left(r_c + \frac{\sigma^2}{2}\right)T}{\sigma\sqrt{T}} \quad d_2 = d_1 - \sigma\sqrt{T}$$

Where:

$S_0$ = initial stock price

$K$ = strike price

$r_c$ = annualized risk-free rate (continuous compounding)

$T$ = time to maturity

If you are not savvy with mathematical notations and the normal distribution portion (d1 and d2) or C = S*N(d1) - Ke^(-r*T)*N(d2). Focus on the stock price minus the strike price, time to expiration and interest rate as the main theme.

Refer to the chart below for a depiction of Call value at expiration:

## Call Option Value at Expiration

▸ $X = \$50$

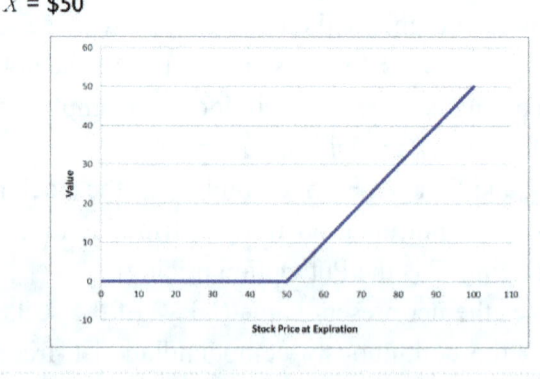

▸ 10                                                        FIN 404

A put option is a contract giving the owner the right, but not the obligation, to sell a specified amount of an underlying security at a pre-determined price within a specified time frame.

For example, if we own a put option that has a contract-specified strike price of $50, we have the right to sell the stock at $50. Even if the stock is worth $25, we can choose to exercise our option and sell the underlying stock at $50 for profit, or allow it to expire in the money also realizing a profit.

Take a look at the PnL graph for a long-put position below, as you can see, the advantage is in your favor if you can keep your emotions in check.

## Put Option Value at Expiration

▸ $X$ = **$50**

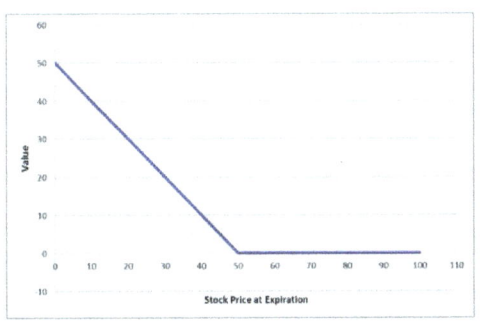

# CHAPTER FOUR

## Time Decay Your New Best Friend

*Time decay is the option's loss in value over time.*
*The only thing that really matters when selling options*

We understand that every option contains two separate components; intrinsic value and time value. Intrinsic value is the difference between the underlying spot price of the stock and the strike price of the option. This is the value of the option if it were to expire immediately. Time value is the difference between the option's intrinsic value and the option's premium. Essentially, this is the value attached to the probability that the intrinsic value will increase prior to expiration. Note: the option premium = IV + TV of the option.

*How do we calculate the time value of an option?*

The time value component of an option is the value of it's worth based on specific probabilities over a specific time period of the stock it is attached too. Time to maturity defines the probability of a price change in the underlying stock. If you give any stock enough time, we expect to see several different price fluctuations. So, as sellers of options, we need to be compensated for the amount of time we give to the buyer.

Longer expiration is always preferable to shorter expiration for American-style call and put options. The value of American call and put options increases with time to expiration, holding all other variables constant. Selling options with an expiration date further out increases the dollar value the seller Note: this chapter and all following chapters will consider American-style options, which can be exercised early (before the expiration date). European options, which do not have this early-exercise feature, are typical of stock-index options and the like.

During the course of an option's life, it's challenging to observe what part of the options price might be coming from loss in time value, as the option's value is affected by multiple variables that are changing at an instantaneous rate. The important thing to remember is that holding all other variables constant, an option's value decreases at an increasing rate as time to maturity approaches.

This phenomenon is called time decay. Typically, an option loses one-third of its time value during the first half of its life and the other two-thirds in the second half of its life. Once the option reaches the last 30 days until expiration, the rate of time decay increases exponentially. This is demonstrated by the graph below.

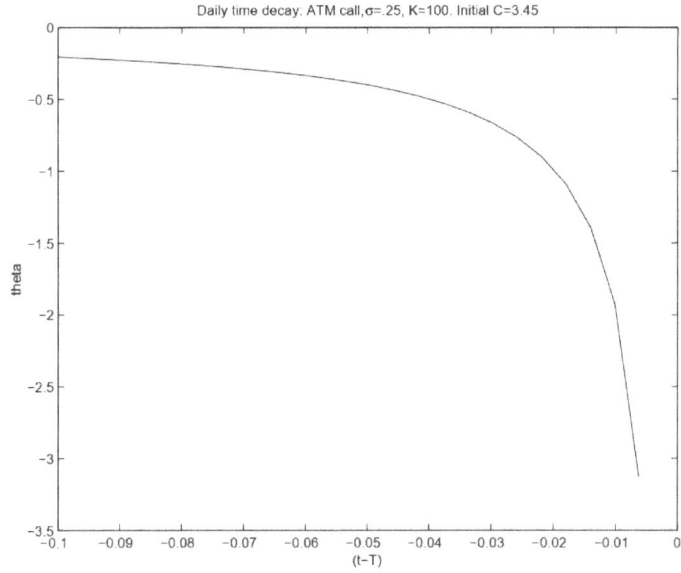

**Value loss in options:**

Let's first look at different hypothetical option value loss scenarios (these are just vague examples to assist the understanding process; however, please note there can be more than one explanation for each scenario).

**Case 1:**

Option value: $5, Value loss: $1, Time period: 5 days

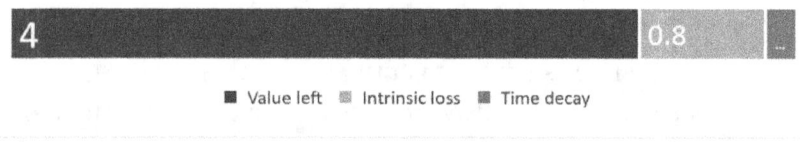

**Closer Look**: Although this option lost $1 in value, we see that only $0.20 of it comes from time value loss in 5 days. So, it lost $0.04 each day throughout 5 days, and it could be that the option was in-the-money $2, but now it's in-the-money $1.20 due to underlying price change.

Option value: $1.5, Value loss: $0.30, Time period: 15 days

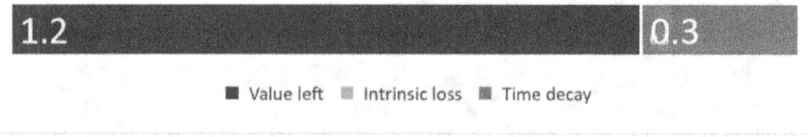

**Closer Look**: Here we don't see any intrinsic value loss throughout the entire 15 days. It is not very likely that the underlying did not change at all during this period, so the best assumption is that this option was already out-of-the-money and had no intrinsic value. A $0.30 time-value loss in 15 days is also not likely to be in the last 15 days to maturity because an option worth $1.50 would lose its value rapidly in those last 15 days.

Option value: $5, Value loss: $1, Time period: 3 days

■ Value left  ▒ Intrinsic loss  ■ Time decay

**Closer Look**: This time we see that time value loss is considerably more. Again, the intrinsic value loss is zero. The scenario is highly likely that the option is reaching its expiration out-of-the-money and time value is decreasing at an increasing rate. Most of the value left is lost in 3 days.

Option value: $25 Value loss: $5.10, Time period: 4 days, Time value loss: $0.04

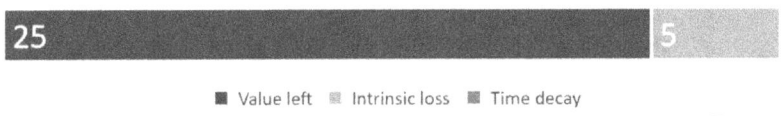

■ Value left  ▒ Intrinsic loss  ■ Time decay

**Closer Look**: It's hard to illustrate on the graphic however, the time value loss is $0.04. Observation period is 4 days and the option has a current value of $25. This suggests that the option is nowhere near its expiration date as it only lost $0.001 per day on average. We also see a $5 loss in value. This is potentially a scenario where the option was in-the-money and still is. However, it lost $5, meaning the underlying price moved in the opposite direction from the strike in those 4 days. More specifically, if it is a put option with a strike price of $150, that means the underlying could quite possibly have gone from $180 to $175, hence losing $5 in intrinsic value. If it was a call option with a strike of $150, it's possible that underlying went from $120 to $125, losing $5 in intrinsic value.

**Mini glossary:**

| | |
|---|---|
| Time value: | Time value is one of the two components of an option's value (the other is intrinsic value) |
| Theta: | Theta is the Greek parameter of an option that is related to time left to maturity.<br>It shows the time value loss of an option per one day.<br>(Also, it is a dynamic value that can change based on other variables) |
| Time decay: | Time decay is the decline of an option's price over time and it's not a linear concept. Time decay is expected to increase as the option approaches its maturity. |

*Time Value vs Intrinsic Value*

Previously we discussed that the time value calculation is influenced by the following factors: in-the-moneyness, time to expiration, risk free interest rate, and volatility.

Let's look at the time value effects of "In-the-moneyness." Given that all of the other parameters are stationary, if an option (call or put) is deep in-the-money, its time value decreases while the intrinsic value increases or decreases based on the movement of the stock. *Time value goes to $0 at the close of the market on the expiration date. At that time, the option is only worth what the intrinsic value is.* If an option is deep out-of-the-money, time value again decreases, and intrinsic value is $0.

However, when an option is at-the-money, its time value has its maximum value while intrinsic value is at $0. The explanation for this is that when an option is at-the-money, the probability of it becoming in-the-money is the highest. This probability is what makes the option's time value the highest out of the three.

Here is another example of an option on AMZN when it's trading at $1523. It's a call option with a maturity date of July 19th, 2019, and a strike price of $1670. Thus, at the start of January 2019, it is out-of-the-money and is trading for $103.

Let's isolate the volatility and interest rate so we can observe the time value more accurately. (Volatility approx. 35%, interest rate, r = 2%)

| AMZN: $1523, Call, Strike: $1670, Vol: 35%, r: 2% | | |
|---|---|---|
| Days to maturity | Price | Theta |
| 197 | 103.73 | -0.24 |
| 150 | 86.44 | -0.29 |
| 120 | 77.63 | -0.34 |
| 90 | 66.54 | -0.38 |
| 60 | 53.82 | -0.47 |
| 30 | 38.00 | -0.72 |
| 20 | 30.50 | -0.77 |
| 10 | 21.69 | -1.08 |
| 5 | 15.33 | -1.52 |
| 1 | 3.43 | -3.41 |

The example above demonstrates the progressive increase in the rate of time decay. Here Theta is showing the daily value loss, so as the time left to maturity decreases, theta becomes a larger value.

You can also see that the price of the option in the first interval drops from $103 to $86 in almost 50 days. However, the last 4-day interval causes a $10+ drop in the price. This non-linear acceleration is a very important characteristic of options. It clearly illustrates the advantage we have as option sellers looking to generate monthly income.

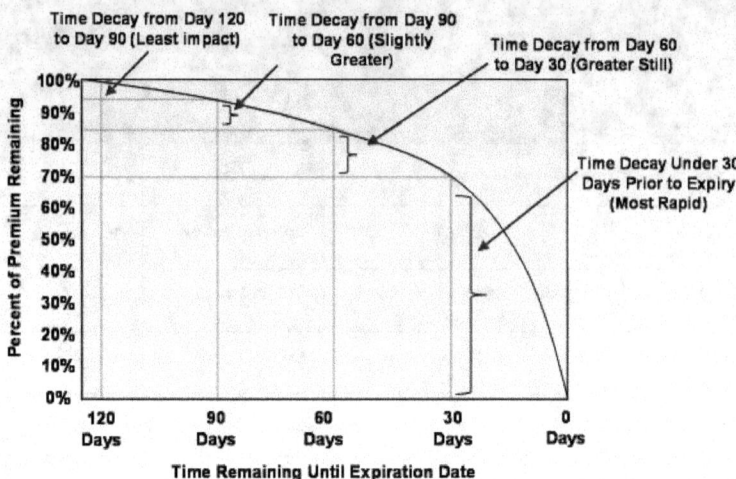

Note the rate at which time premium begins to decay is roughly 30 days prior to expiration. We can see that theta is not a linear progression as the option advances toward expiration. Rather, options closer to expiration will decay at an exponentially increasing rate as time to maturity decreases.

# CHAPTER FIVE

## Implied Volatility

Volatility is an important input in the formula that is used for pricing options. It shows the magnitude of the variance that exists in the prices of an underlying security over a period of time. With that being said, how accurately can you predict the future based on the historical data? Let's take a closer look to understand some of the theoretical and practical concepts that help investment professionals enable the use of this powerful estimation tool.

## VOLATILITY STATISTICS:

The most basic approach to calculate the volatility of a data set is by calculating the variance using its square root, the outcome is its standard deviation.

If we are looking to calculate the variance for a period of 15 days, we need to calculate the mean deviation of each day's specific stock prices. The second step is to square those deviations then divide the sum by the number of data items (in this case, 15). This will give us the variation. Although it is simple math, it can be confusing and tedious for newcomers. Thankfully using today's technology, spreadsheets help a great deal with such calculations.

The standard deviation that is derived from taking the square-root of each point's variance from the mean is the volatility input. This input is used in the Black-Scholes option pricing model.

When volatility is calculated by this standard deviation method, it is called historical volatility (i.e. using historical price returns and taking each return's variance from the mean, squaring that number, summing all of them, and then taking the square-root of the sum). See below:

$$\sigma = \sqrt{\frac{\sum_{i=1}^{n}(r_i - \mu)^2}{n - 1}}$$

Where:

$\sigma$ = Standard deviation
$r_i$ = Price returns
$\mu$ = Mean (average) of all data points
$n$ = Number of data points

Note:

$$\mu = \sum_{i=1}^{n} r_i \quad \text{and} \quad r_i = \frac{(P_{i+1} - P_i)}{i}$$

Historical volatility example:

**Let's look at S&P 500 price data for a 15-day period.**

| | Date | Close / Last | Mean Deviation | Deviation Squared |
|---|---|---|---|---|
| 1 | 1/4/2019 | 252.39 | 2 | 6.2 |
| 2 | 1/3/2019 | 244.21 | -6 | 32.3 |
| 3 | 1/2/2019 | 250.18 | 0 | 0.1 |
| 4 | 12/31/2018 | 249.92 | 0 | 0.0 |
| 5 | 12/28/2018 | 247.75 | -2 | 4.6 |
| 6 | 12/27/2018 | 248.07 | -2 | 3.3 |
| 7 | 12/26/2018 | 246.18 | -4 | 13.8 |
| 8 | 12/24/2018 | 234.34 | -16 | 242.0 |
| 9 | 12/21/2018 | 240.70 | -9 | 84.6 |
| 10 | 12/20/2018 | 247.17 | -3 | 7.4 |
| 11 | 12/19/2018 | 251.26 | 1 | 1.9 |
| 12 | 12/18/2018 | 255.08 | 5 | 26.9 |
| 13 | 12/17/2018 | 255.36 | 5 | 29.8 |
| 14 | 12/14/2018 | 260.47 | 11 | 111.8 |
| 15 | 12/13/2018 | 265.37 | 15 | 239.4 |
| | | Mean: | Average of Prices | 250 |
| | | Variance: | Average of Dev. Sq. | 53.6 |
| | | Standard Dev. | Sq. Root of Variance | 7.32 |

Averages (interchangeable with "mean") in the example above can be calculated with a simple =Average formula. The mathematical foundation of this formula is summing each data point and dividing the total by the number of observations.

Similarly, you can use Standard Deviation and/or variance formulas to calculate the needed values directly in Excel.

Although it is a very useful concept, historical volatility can be misleading because markets frequently change in unpredictable ways.

*Shortcomings of historical volatility:*

Historical volatility inherits an assumption that history will always repeat itself. Although this is true to a certain extent, there are always price movements and historical events that surprise even the most seasoned investment professionals. Historical volatility works well when predicting small price changes and trends over longer periods of time.

However, historical volatility is useless in predicting large directional changes in price. When something like this occurs, volatility immediately jumps significantly higher because of the change in deviation from the mean. If you are selling options against a stock and the implied volatility (i.e. the volatility "implied" by the market) on those options spike, you will want to sell your options and collect the higher premium. If you have already sold your calls, a spike in implied volatility will make it considerably more expensive to buy the call options back. In this case, the best thing to do is nothing – remember that these options may become cheaper due to time decay and regardless of that, our overall trading goal is to generate monthly income.

Other phenomena, even more unexpected, are black swan events. They were successfully theorized by economist Nassim Taleb and they define events that are greatly beyond normal expectations of science, politics, technology, markets, etc. From this definition, we understand that if a topic is being widely discussed and predicted by many people, then it is not a black swan. Black swans catch everyone by surprise and are extremely unexpected in nature. **Emotional tip**

Since the historical data is not always a reliable metric to estimate future volatility of an asset, what can be used to reinforce the future price predictions? Although it is an imperfect solution, implied volatility is a popular alternative to use in volatility calculations.

## IMPLIED VOLATILITY

Implied volatility, a.k.a. the "market volatility" of an asset is calculated by taking current option prices in the market and reverse-engineering the volatility input from those prices. Since an option's strike price, underlying price, interest rate, and time to expiration are certain values, it is relatively simple to use several iterations and extract an implied volatility value.

There are benefits and shortcomings of implied volatility. First, by checking the daily average movement of the market or stock, you are able to tell any volatility measures that are different than the theoretical historical volatility calculations. Thus, you can judge the potential future volatility of a stock or index by looking at the implied volatility of its options.

On the other hand, this can cause a *"herd mentality"* as everyone rushes to buy that option therefore driving the price higher than normal. If many people start judging the volatility only by implied volatility, this will create a closed-loop feedback system where everyone is relying on the same implied volatility values. For this reason, it is very important for option traders to remain critical as they calculate values for volatility; remember that these values are only an estimation of actual volatility.

Another important and fundamental point to keep in mind is that volatility doesn't tell us the direction of price movements in a stock. Generally, in a flat market, a move in either direction would increase the volatility, thus causing a change in option values (all else constant).

## Mini Glossary

| | |
|---|---|
| Volatility: | A concept to measure the magnitude of price fluctuations. |
| Types of Volatility: | Historical, implied, stochastic |
| Other names: | Vol., IV (implied volatility), HV (historical volatility) |
| Symbol: | $\sigma$<br>(Sigma) |
| Greek: | $\Upsilon$<br>(Vega) |
| Volatility Indices: | S&P 500 Volatility Index (VIX)<br>S&P 100 Volatility Index (VXO)<br>Nasdaq 100 Volatility Index (VXN) |

Knowledge Tip: What's the volatility change on a stock that is increasing 2% every day? (In a 90-day range)

The answer would be zero. Since a stock maintains the same level of change on a day-to-day basis, the variance and standard deviation would remain the same.

## VOLATILITY INDICES:

There are volatility index's that are calculated by The CBOE Global Markets® (CBOE®). You can also find options and futures that use these index's as underlying securities.

**US Volatility Indices**                                     Delayed Quotes (7/1/2019)

| Ticker | Index | Sym | Last | Pt. Change |
|--------|-------|-----|------|------------|
| VIX® | Cboe Volatility Index® | VIX | 22.60 | -2.54 |
| VXN^SM | Cboe NASDAQ Volatility Index | VXN | 28.57 | 0.00 |
| VXO^SM | Cboe S&P 100 Volatility Index | VXO | 24.38 | 0.00 |
| VXD^SM | Cboe DJIA Volatility Index | VXD | 22.16 | 0.00 |
| RVX^SM | Cboe Russell 2000 Volatility Index | RVX | 25.30 | 0.00 |

**Volatility Indices on Non-U.S. Stock ETFs**             Delayed Quotes

| Ticker | Index | Sym | Last | Pt. Change |
|--------|-------|-----|------|------------|
| VXEFA | Cboe EFA ETF Volatility Index | VXEFA | 18.07 | 0.00 |
| VXEEM | Cboe Emerging Markets ETF Volatility Index | VXEEM | 23.86 | 0.00 |
| VXFXI | Cboe China ETF Volatility Index | VXFXI | 25.03 | 0.00 |
| VXEWZ | Cboe Brazil ETF Volatility Index | VXEWZ | 34.57 | 0.00 |

**Volatility Indices on Interest Rates:**          Delayed Quotes

| Ticker | Index | Sym | Last | Pt. Change |
|--------|-------|-----|------|------------|
| TYVIX | Cboe/CBOT 10-year U.S. Treasury Note Volatility Index | TYVIX | 4.63 | 0.00 |
| SRVIX | Cboe Interest Rate Swap Volatility Index | SRVIX | 74.32 | 0.00 |

**Volatility Indices on Commodity-related ETF's:**          Delayed Quotes

| Ticker | Index | Sym | Last | Pt. Change |
|--------|-------|-----|------|------------|
| OVX | Cboe Crude Oil ETF Volatility Index | OVX | 51.52 | 0.00 |
| GVZ | Cboe Gold ETF Volatility Index | GVZ | 12.04 | 0.00 |
| VXSLV | Cboe Silver ETF Volatility Index | VXSLV | 21.70 | 0.00 |
| VXGDX | Cboe Gold Miners ETF Volatility Index | VXGDX | 31.76 | 0.00 |
| VXXLE | Cboe Energy Sector ETF Volatility Index | VXXLE | 29.95 | 0.00 |

**Volatility Indices on Currency-related Futures/ETF's:**          Delayed Quotes

| Ticker | Index | Sym | Last | Pt. Change |
|--------|-------|-----|------|------------|
| EUVIX | Cboe/CME FX Euro Volatility IndexSM | EUVIX | 6.96 | 0.00 |
| JYVIX | Cboe/CME FX Yen Volatility IndexSM | JYVIX | 9.48 | 0.00 |
| BPVIX | Cboe/CME FX British Pound Volatility IndexSM | BPVIX | 13.03 | 0.00 |
| Evz | Cboe Eurocurrency ETF Volatility Index | Evz | 7.29 | 0.00 |

**Volatility Indices on Single Stocks:**    Delayed Quotes

| Ticker | Index | Sym | Last | Pt. Change |
|--------|-------|-----|------|-----------|
| VXAZN | Cboe Equity VIX® on Amazon | VXAZN | 44.38 | 0.00 |
| VXAPL | Cboe Equity VIX® on Apple | VXAPL | 37.55 | 0.00 |
| VXGS | Cboe Equity VIX® on Goldman Sachs | VXGS | 36.60 | 0.00 |
| VXGOG | Cboe Equity VIX® on Google | VXGOG | 33.35 | 0.00 |
| VXIBM | Cboe Equity VIX® on IBM | VXIBM | 34.86 | 0.00 |

**Volatility of VIX:**    Delayed Quotes

| Ticker | Index | Sym | Last | Pt. Change |
|--------|-------|-----|------|-----------|
| VVIX | Cboe VIX of VIX Index | VVIX | 84.44 | 0.00 |

Source: The Chicago Board Options Exchange Website (CBOE.com)

*Volatility – ETF Symbol = VXX – My Personal Favorite*

*This is the only option I buy in my personal account and there is a very specific reason why…I have no idea when it's going to spike a market sell off, however since I know the spike is caused by the implied volatility of the S&P 500 front month put options I know those put options will eventually revert back to the mean and the VXX will as well. To put it in simple terms – when the market starts to pull back every novice trader goes out and buys put contracts on the S&P 500 – the VXX tracks the pricing of those puts and we just learned that implied volatility is simply the herd running from the lions which causes the price to go up. Give it a day or two and buy the following week ATM or ITM puts. As the market stabilizes and that protection those individual's we mentioned earlier begins to collapse we would like to be on the put contract side. Never buy the calls unless you are hedging your portfolio when the market is at all-time highs. The people who bought the puts when the market pulled back or crashed bought at SUPER high prices.*

# VEGA

Let's look at an option based on the NASDAQ 100 index, which tracks the top 100 stocks that are listed on the Nasdaq stock exchange. The PowerShares ETF QQQ ticker is an ETF based on the Nasdaq 100. While the Nasdaq 100 is just an abstract index calculation, QQQ can be bought and sold, thus trading the same way an individual stock trades.

There are options based on QQQ; let's analyze a few of them. As the underlying QQQ was trading around $156 that day, both options are at-the-money.

**Option1:** Mar 15, 2019 156.00 Call (@QQQ) is a call option with strike price of 156 and maturity date of 15th of March 2019.

**Technical parameters**

Delta0.79563
Gamma0.03777
Rho0.21642
Theta-0.10059
Vega0.18640

**Option2:** Mar 15, 2019 156.00 Put (@QQQ) is a put option
with strike price of 156 and maturity date of 15th of March 2019.

**Technical parameters**

Delta-0.41405
Gamma0.02203
Rho-0.07932
Theta-0.04495
Vega0.24704

The call option has a Vega of 0.186, this means a 1% change of volatility in the underlying price causes $0.186 price change in the option. If volatility increased by 10%, the call price would increase $1.86 in value (all else constant).

The put option, on the other hand, has a Vega of 0.247. Although volatility affects option pricing the same in both put and call options, Vega is higher here, therefore a 1% increase in the volatility would cause the option price to increase $0.247. The logic behind this difference is the thought that markets tend to sell off much more quickly and violently.

## More advanced approaches

One big criticism with the Black-Scholes model is that it assumes volatility is constant throughout the life of the option. Although this was still a breakthrough in mathematics for option pricing, obviously we understand that volatility is not a constant value. In fact, it changes at an instantaneous rate! Stochastic Volatility (SV) is one of the answers to this shortcoming of the other measures of volatility.

# CHAPTER SIX

## The Greeks

Option Greeks represent sensitivity of an option's price. Each Greek is the sensitivity measurement for a variable that affects the option's price directly in Black & Scholes formula.

|  | Theta | Delta | Gamma | Rho | Vega |
|---|---|---|---|---|---|
| Greek symbol: | Θ | Δ | Γ | P | V |
| Sensitivity to: | Time to Maturity | Underlying Price Change | Underlying Price Change | Interest Rate Change | Volatility Change |
| Affects: | Option price | Option price | Delta | Option price | Option price |

Option Greeks measure sensitivity to variables that are used in the option price calculations, such as underlying price, volatility, interest rate, and time to maturity.

# DELTA (D)

Delta is the sensitivity of an option's price to the change in the underlying asset's price. If delta is 0.5, this means a price change of $1 in the underlying price will cause a price change of $0.50 in the option's price. If the option is a call, then option price moves in the same direction and if the option is a put, then the delta will affect the option price in the opposite direction than the underlying price.

Note that call deltas range from 0 to 1.0 (thus an at-the-money call option has a delta of 0.50) and put deltas range from 0.0 to -1.0 (thus an at-the-money put option has a delta of -0.50). We will cover some examples to elaborate on this.

# GAMMA (C)

Gamma is the only second-order Greek that we will cover in this book, meaning it is a Greek of a Greek. It is the only commonly utilized second-order Greek, as well. It shows the option's delta change per $1 change in the underlying asset price.

# VEGA (V)

Another important Greek is Vega, which shows the sensitivity to the volatility and option value increases parallel to the volatility of the underlying asset. Vega implications are the same for both calls and puts; this is because an increase in volatility causes an increase in option price regardless of its type.

# THETA (I)

Theta describes the sensitivity or change in an option's value based on the time remaining to expiration. In this case, as we sell the call options, we collect the theta value from the buyer up front. As time passes, the time value of any option decreases, meaning we are profiting from the time value decline of the option we sold.

In other words, we sell the option when theta is high, and profit as it goes all the way down to zero at maturity. This is a fundamental concept of insurance as well, and that's the reason why if you'd like to insure your car, your house, your life, or anything, the greater the duration the more the insurance will cost. If nothing bad happens during the insurance period, the insurer realizes the premium you have paid.

# RHO (R)

Rho is used to measure sensitivity to an interest rate change. Assume that a call option is currently priced at $10 and has a rho value of 0.5, if the interest rates increase by 1%, then the call option price will increase by $0.50 (to $10.50) or by the amount of its rho value. Usually you don't want interest rates to increase after you sold your call option as you will have sold at a cheaper price. However, small interest rate fluctuations shouldn't be significant unless you have a very big position. This is the least important Greek to worry about, but it is still important to know.

**Option Greek example:**
Apple Inc. Feb 22, 2019, 148.00 (@AAPL) Call & Put
(At-the-money on 7/1/2019, AAPL stock: $148)

| Call | Put |
| --- | --- |
| Delta 0.63829 | Delta -0.43156 |
| Gamma 0.03090 | Gamma 0.02287 |
| Rho 0.11032 | Rho -0.05734 |
| Theta -0.11973 | Theta -0.06968 |
| Vega 0.19138 | Vega 0.19733 |
| Impvol 0.24997 | Impvol 0.40894 |

In the example, we see that the call option has a delta of $0.64 and the put option has a delta of $0.43, meaning if AAPL stock price went up $1, the call option would increase $0.64 and the put option price would decrease $0.43.

We also see that the call option has a gamma of 0.03 and the put option has a gamma of 0.02. This means that if the AAPL stock increases $1 in price, the call's delta will increase to 0.66 and the put option's delta will increase to -0.45.

Rho for the call seems to be 0.110 and for the put, -0.057. This means a 1% of interest rate increase is expected to cause a $0.11 increase in the call's price and $0.057 decrease in the put's price.

Theta shows the price decrease over a daily time frame. It appears as though the call option is losing $0.119 every day that passes and the put option is losing $0.06968 every day that passes. Also, as the time to maturity changes, theta is expected to change solely based on that, as well.

Finally, Vega of 0.19 each shows us that a 1% increase in the underlying price of volatility will cause and increase of 0.19% in both options' price. A 1% decrease in volatility would cause a decrease of both option prices by $0.19.

Having good knowledge of first-order Greeks will give you a great base to understanding option behaviors and successfully trading them. It is also good to keep in mind that Greeks are not constant values and they change as parameters that affect the option prices change.

Implied volatility and time decay have been covered in detail in dedicated chapters. You now can find very useful knowledge in these chapters that also give a deeper insight regarding Greeks, vega, and theta, respectively.

# CHAPTER SEVEN

## Covered Call's Generate Monthly Income

*"One of the funny things about the stock market is that
every time one person buys, another person sells, and both think
they are astute." -William Feather*

In creating a strong portfolio that uses all the tools available to us for
writing contracts, we might consider...for a moment...the game of
golf. Golfers often feel they are better at the short game or the long
game. Few golfers feel they are equally proficient at both. According
to Golfweek, "The game of golf can be broken down into two ele-
ments: the long game and the short game. In the long game, power
and distance are required so that the player's ball can approach the
putting green in as few strokes as possible. In the short game, the
skills needed are more finesse-related due to the need for accuracy. In
order to be a successful golfer, a player must master both aspects of
the game."

Similarly, those of us writing contracts will find our area of expertise. There are a number of ways to write contracts that provide
for higher levels of success, if understood and used correctly. Briefly,
these are covered calls, poor man's covered calls, selling puts, and
iron condors. These strategies are popular, specific approaches to options trading. Most often, as with the short game or long game in golf,
each of us will find that certain ways of writing contracts will appeal
to us and others won't appeal to us.

Covered calls are one of the most common options trading strategies used to generate monthly income, reduce portfolio risk, and create trading opportunities.

A covered call is nothing but a position of a long stock (or another underlying product) and short call option combined. It allows us to benefit from upward and downward movements in a stock and choose outcomes that are beneficial given our expectations of the market.

## COVERED CALL BENEFITS:

The writer of the covered call is paid the premium in cash in exchange for relinquishing their possible increase in the stock price, which would allow them to cash it out at a higher price. In essence, the contract writer is selling the future benefits of the stock. For example, let's assume you buy Apple stocks for $250 per share, because you are sure that the stock price is going to go up to $350 over the next six months.

However, as someone who enjoys cash profits, you might consider selling the stock sooner if you can achieve even a $50 dollar increase in the stock's price and taking the profits earlier. In other words, those of us who write contracts may lose a bit on the long end, but we have the bird-in-the-hand cash to provide us with mortgage payment cash and other bill paying cash. This is the primary reason that contract writers find what they do to be appealing.

Figure 8.1 demonstrates how our covered call strategy (in green) reacts to the price differences in the market. The stock and short call position have their own, somewhat opposite, reactions to the movement in the market. If you recall, a call option is a bullish bet that gives the option buyer the right to purchase a stock at a pre-defined price (strike price) at a specific date in the future.

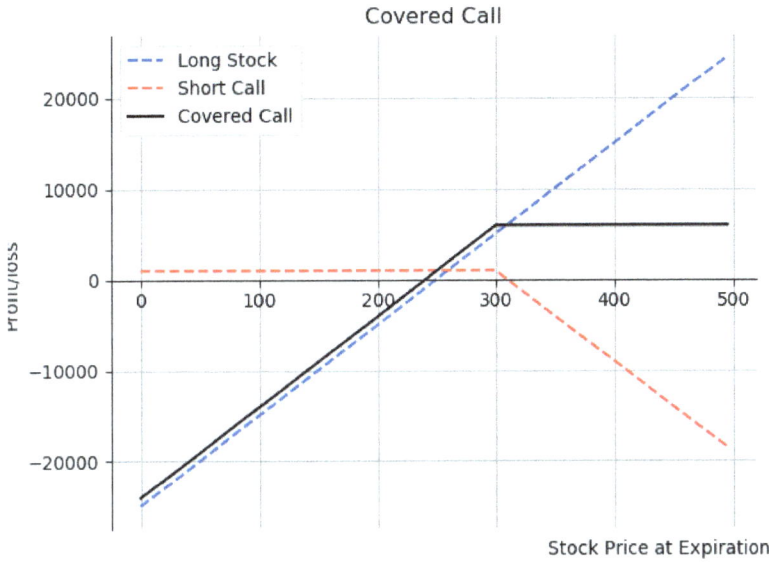

**Figure 8.1: Typical profit profile of a covered call position.**

What happens if the underlying price in the stock rises? Remember, you sold them the right to purchase your stock at a pre-defined price on a specific date in the future, so, if the underlying stock skyrockets, you owe them the difference (between the strike price and the price that you paid for the stock originally). When the stock price increases (horizontal axis), the blue and red lines converge; if the stock continues to move higher it will rise above your strike price.

The covered call represented by the solid black line is the income you generated on day one that you can use to live on.

On the other end of the spectrum, you will profit from the difference between your cost of underlying stock and strike price if you are assigned on the expiration date. Also, consider the fact that 75% of all options expire worthless; it is likely (although not guaranteed) that you collected premium and have no need to worry as the call options you sold expire worthless.

In summary, selling covered calls to generate monthly income gives you the ability sell call options, collect your profit on day one and only obligate yourself to sell your shares at a higher price in the future. As stock prices tend to rise over the long term, implementing a covered call strategy is inherently more likely to make you money if you repeat the process month after month.

Basic calculations

| Value | Formula |
|---|---|
| Cost Basis of Covered Call | Stock Price – Call Premium |
| Maximum Profit | (Stock Price/Cost Basis) – 1 |
| Downside Protection | 1 – (Cost Basis/Stock Price) |

**Figure 8.3**

Cost Basis of Covered Call: This value shows us the amount of cost for our covered call. Basically, as we purchase the underlying stock and short the call options on the same stock, our cost is stock price minus option premium.

Maximum Profit: Covered call is a capped strategy in terms of profits. Share count multiplied by the strike price plus premium collected is the maximum profit you can realize.

Downside Protection: Premium collected divided by number of shares equals a "per-share value" this is the value that the stock would need to lose before hitting your principle.

***Important Greeks of Covered Calls:***

All investors might not be interested in knowing the detailed technical aspects of derivatives such as the Greeks, especially in their raw forms. However, in certain situations, they provide great insight to the nature of your investment and what call option you decide to sell.

Keep in mind that the Greeks are sensitivity values, they will change as other parameters change, such as underlying price, volatility, interest rate and time to maturity.

## DELTA (D)

Recall from the previous chapter that the delta of an option is the sensitivity of an option's value per $1 change in the underlying asset's price. One of the big advantages of covered calls here is that you usually start with a delta-neutral position, meaning your short calls are covered with the underlying asset you are holding, so ideally you would be neutral to delta and gamma of the covered call if it is done properly.

## VEGA (V)

Recall that vega is the measurement of an option's price sensitivity to changes in the volatility of the underlying asset. As you are selling a call option with this strategy, you don't want the volatility to increase after you sold your calls as you will have sold your option for less premium than it will be in the market if volatility moves higher. Volatility is a major component in option price calculations, we will touch on that a little more deeply in other chapters.

If you are a veteran trader, you might want to close your short option position if the volatility falls after getting in a covered call position, since the option prices will be cheaper now and you have the opportunity to close your short call position by buying the same options at a lower price.

## THETA (I)

Theta describes the sensitivity or change in an option's value based on the time remaining to expiration. The rate of change will vary depending on the time remaining, this is called time decay. When we sell the call option, we collect up front the theta value from the buyer. As time passes, the time value of every option decreases, this means we will realize the profit from the time value component of the option we sold.

## RHO (R)

Usually we don't want interest rates to increase after selling the call option, because you will have sold at a cheaper price than necessary. However, small interest rate fluctuations won't make a difference unless you are dealing with extremely large position sizes.

## OUT-OF-THE-MONEY COVERED CALLS

Simply, if the call options being shorted are out-of-the-money, this is referred to as an "out-of-the-money covered call." As out-of-the-money options have no intrinsic value and only time value, they cost less. This means we will collect a lower premium on the call option we sold.

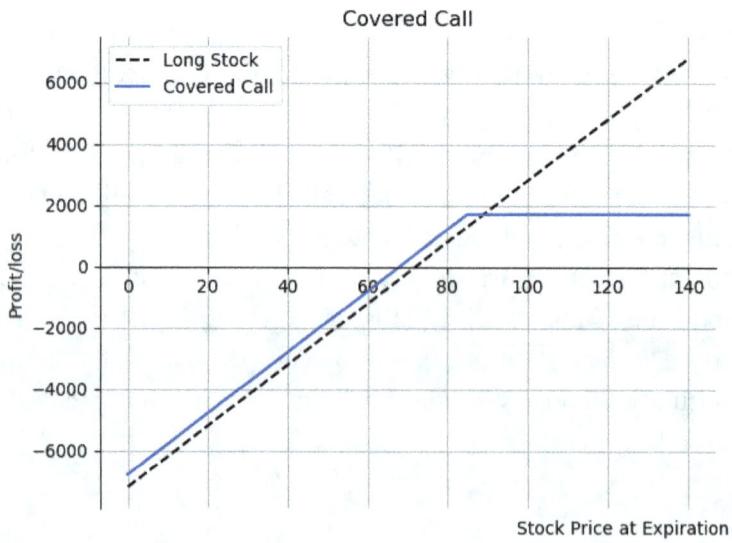

**Advantage**: Larger profit potential

## An example:
## 3 Scenarios:

(Let's use an example where you've bought TESLA stock at $319 one month ago and sold the $350 strike price TESLA calls today. Let's also say you sold your call options at $11.00 per contract, with a term of 120 days, volatility around 30% and risk-free interest rate of 2.5%. (Remember 1 contract equals 100 shares of stock)

120 days later…

**Underlying price doesn't go past $350 at maturity:**
You end up pocketing the profits from the call premium and still own the stock that you presumably wouldn't mind owning. (Meaning you're not bearish on the stock)

**Underlying price goes past $350 at maturity:**
You pocket profits from your call premiums (i.e.: 11 x 100 = $1100). In addition, you will also deliver the TESLA stocks at $350, which you bought at $319, your share price gain is $350 - $319 = $31 x 100 = $3100. Total Profit is calculated by adding the two values together $1100 + $3100 = $4200

**Underlying price goes down below $319 at maturity:**
In this case, obviously your market insight was in the wrong direction. Normally you would lose money instantly with conventional trading strategies. However, with covered calls you won't lose as much, and the stock will need to drop below what you collected in income on day one. The $1100 premium collected will act as a buffer on your stock holding. The 319 – 11 = $308 is your breakeven and only past that level will you start losing money on your stocks.

Knowledge tip: Out-of-the-money means the call option's strike price is above the current market price of the underlying asset, when you sell an out-of-the-money call you are collecting the time value of that option since there is no intrinsic value.

## IN-THE-MONEY COVERED CALLS

Opposite to the "out-of-the-money covered calls," the call option component of our strategy is in-the-money, this creates more room for protection of profits in the case of a price fall. So, when you sell an in-the-money call you are expecting no upside and potentially short-term downside movement. Selling "in-the-money calls" is a way to lock in share price profits and collect some premium while doing it.

However, it will have much more room on the negative side as underlying price falls. Your profit is likely to stay flat for a while before you start losing from the profits (collected premiums) and only after a certain price level your strategy will reach the break even and go into the loss zone. The same strategy with out-of-the-money covered call strategy won't give you that much room for the underlying asset to fall.

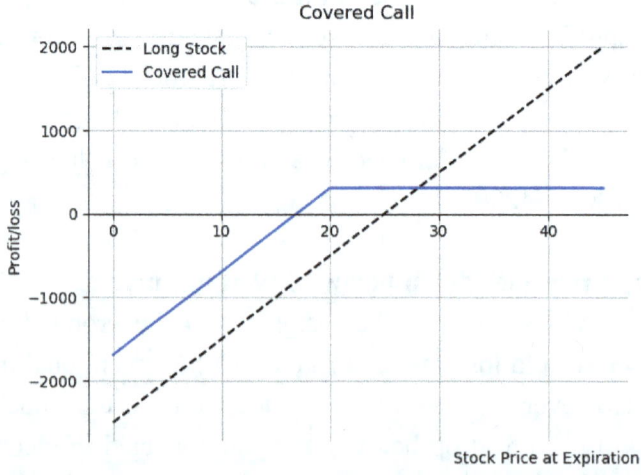

**Figure 8.5**

**Advantage**: Less profit opportunity

**Disadvantage**: More protection on the downside (still unlimited loss potential)

**Knowledge tip**: In-the-money means the calls strike price is below the market price of underlying asset.

**3 Scenarios**:
(Let's use an example with in-the-money call options to illustrate the different effects. Let's say you've written $275 TESLA calls and still owned TESLA stock at $319 (the original price you paid for it). Let's also say you sold your call options at $50 per contract, with a term of 120 days, volatility around 30% and risk-free interest rate of 2.50%. As you can see, this option is deep in-the-money and increased intrinsic value makes it a more expensive option.

120 days later…

**Underlying price goes below $319 at maturity**:
You end up pocketing the profits from the call premium (which you keep from day one and is the monthly income we have been discussing) $50 x 100 = $5000. Regardless of the price between the range of $275 and $319, you originally bought the shares at $319 and then you sold the call option at the strike price of $275, which will be assigned on expiration. However, it doesn't matter if the price is $300 or $280 for you as your entry and exit are the same, $319 and $275, respectively. So, 275 - 319 = -$44 x 100 = -$4400 + $5000 (premiums collected) = $600 (limited upside)

**Underlying price goes up past $319 at maturity**:
275 - 319 = -$44 x 100 = -$4400 + $5000 (premiums collected) = $600 (limited upside)

**Underlying price goes below $275 at maturity**:
In this case, obviously, your market insight was deep in the wrong direction, considering you bought the shares at $319 each. But you have way more room before you start losing money. First you collected 50 x 100 = $5000 from call option premiums. They will let you resist any loss all the way until 319 – 50 = $269

As you can see from this example, the upside is much more limited compared to the out-of-the-money call. However, we had a much bigger buffer on the downside, as well.

If you believe the stock is volatile and likely to fall as well as rise, but you don't think it would fall below a certain level due to the stock's fundamental value, this might be a great defensive strategy.

**Executive Summary:**

| | |
|---|---|
| Market direction: | Limited upside or flat |
| Complexity: | Intermediate |
| Risk profile: | Medium to Conservative |
| Capital intensity: | Medium |
| Duration: | Flexible |
| Markets: | Any asset with available options (Usually stocks) |
| Types: | Out-of-the-money & In-the-money |

# CHAPTER EIGHT

## Poor Man's Covered Calls

Covered call writing involves first buying a stock or exchange-traded fund (ETF) and then selling call options on those shares. Each contract we sell requires us to buy 100 shares of the underlying. This can be a challenge for some investors who may look for stock substitutes that will lower cost basis and risk. Enter the Poor Man's Covered Call (PMCC).

This is a covered call-like strategy where a long-term option (LEAPS) is purchased in lieu of a stock. Short-term calls are then sold against the LEAPS. The long call gives the option buyer the right to buy the shares at the strike price by the expiration date. Options cost a lot less than shares of stock, so the cost basis and cash required are reduced as is the risk.

The technical term for this strategy is 'long call diagonal debit spread.' Remember that in this strategy, we simultaneously purchase and sell an equal number of call options on a specific underlying security, with different strike prices and different expiration dates.

Since this is more of a long-term commitment than traditional covered call writing (it's more like portfolio overwriting) we are more likely to consider blue chip stocks like those found in the Dow 30, for example. ETFs with similar underlying qualities (like the SelectSector SPDRs, for example) can also be considered. For our initial setup, low beta stocks in a low volatility environment will establish the most solid foundation to initiate these trades.

Purchasing a LEAP will replace the underlying stock component of a covered call. Thus, it is important to choose the LEAP wisely. Ideally, we want to purchase the LEAP and allow it to move higher over time as the underlying stock moves higher. High delta (coming from the in-the-moneyness) and long-term expiration date will be the key characteristics we are looking for in the LEAP that we buy to replace the stock.

## LEAPS

Long Term Equity Anticipation Securities (LEAPS) are defined as options with a remaining time value until expiration of twelve months or more.

Recall from our discussion on time decay that option's time value depreciates faster during the second half of its life as opposed to the first half. This time value loss accelerates as the option's expiration date approaches. So, buying an option with a long shelf life does not lose as much time value since you are buying it twelve to twenty-four months before expiration. The time value losses will be very insignificant when compared to the time value losses that will occur in the later stages of the option's life. This is one of the characteristics of LEAPS that allow them to more closely track the equity's characteristics and price movements.

One of the most important data points to look at prior to purchasing a LEAP is the Greek calculation delta. If you recall, delta is the sensitivity to the stock's price change and its effects on the options price. LEAPS that are further in-the-money tend to have higher deltas which allows it to more closely imitate the stock's price changes. A delta of 1 perfectly simulates the underlying price change in the option price with a 1 to 1 ratio, however, an /option with 0.50 delta will only change by fifty cents in relation to a one dollar move in the underlying stock.

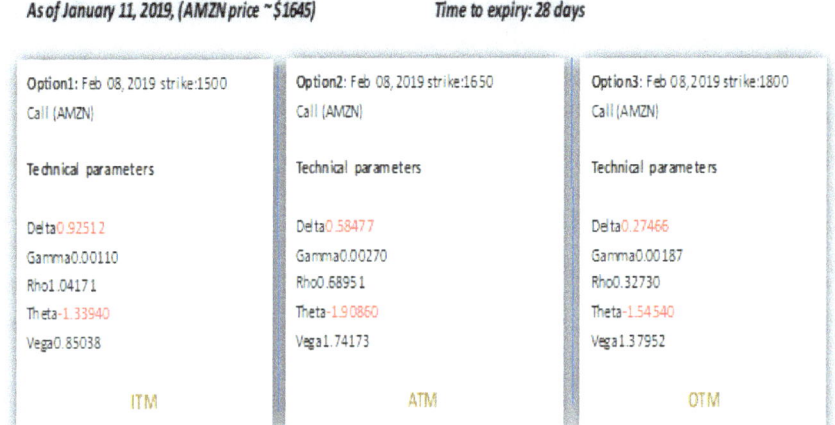

**As of January 11, 2019, (AMZN price ~$1645)**          **Time to expiry: 28 days**

| Option1: Feb 08, 2019 strike:1500 | Option2: Feb 08, 2019 strike:1650 | Option3: Feb 08, 2019 strike:1800 |
|---|---|---|
| Call (AMZN) | Call (AMZN) | Call (AMZN) |
| Technical parameters | Technical parameters | Technical parameters |
| Delta 0.92512 | Delta 0.58477 | Delta 0.27466 |
| Gamma 0.00110 | Gamma 0.00270 | Gamma 0.00187 |
| Rho 1.04171 | Rho 0.68951 | Rho 0.32730 |
| Theta -1.33940 | Theta -1.90860 | Theta -1.54540 |
| Vega 0.85038 | Vega 1.74173 | Vega 1.37952 |
| ITM | ATM | OTM |

## In Option 1

You can observe in-the-money options parameters and how the strike price directly effects the time value of an option. In the first box you will see we selected the $1500-dollar strike price which is $145 dollars ITM with 28 days till expiration. Buying deep in-the-money calls increases the Delta while simultaneously decreasing the time decay or Theta. Theta is the lowest for the deep in-the-money option since the time value is making up a very small portion of the options value while Delta is highest because the intrinsic value makes up the majority of the options true value.

## In Option 2

You will notice the delta decreases as we move our strike price up and closer to where Amazon is trading at in the open market because we have very little if any intrinsic value. Theta (time decay) is highest here because the inherent mechanics of options place the highest dollar time value for options that are at-the-money (ATM).

## In Option 3

represents the scenario that we will be implementing when we do a covered call as well as a PMCC. You will see that the further away your strike price the lower the delta. Time Value is higher here because it's the only value the option has right now. The time value is calculated with the information we listed above but for this example Amazon tends to have more volatility on a daily basis so it's not uncommon to see the Theta be that high.

The three examples above illustrate how the Greeks on an option change based on the (in-the-money, at-the-money, and out-of-the-money, respectively). All three examples represent real data on Amazon and have the same time left to maturity (28 days).

The three examples below illustrate how the Greeks on an option change based on the (in-the-money, at-the-money, and out-of-the-money, respectively). All three examples represent real data on Amazon and have the same time left to maturity (371 days). As you can see, the difference in days left until expiration, as well as, the strike price selected drastically changes the expected movement and price change of the same option.

*As of January 11, 2019, (AMZN price ~$1645)*　　　　*Time to expiry: 371 days*

| Option1: Jan 17, 2019 strike:1500 Call (AMZN) | Option2: Jul 19, 2019 strike:1650 Call (AMZN) | Option3: Jul 19, 2019 strike:1800 Call (AMZN) |
|---|---|---|
| Technical parameters | Technical parameters | Technical parameters |
| Delta 1.00000 | Delta 0.99124 | Delta 0.61821 |
| Gamma 0.00000 | Gamma 0.00040 | Gamma 0.00173 |
| Rho 6.85872 | Rho 7.48046 | Rho 4.68552 |
| Theta -0.95925 | Theta -1.05103 | Theta -0.93057 |
| Vega 0.00000 | Vega 0.36468 | Vega 5.13321 |
| ITM | ATM | OTM |

Below you will find a graph to further demonstrate Delta's relationship with the intrinsic value. In order to implement this strategy, you need to buy a LEAP (call option that has twelve months or more to expiration). Ideally, we would select an option with a high Delta so the option we own moves as close to $1 to $1 with the stock. Remember, Deltas value show us that if our stock goes up one dollar our call option goes up one dollar as well.

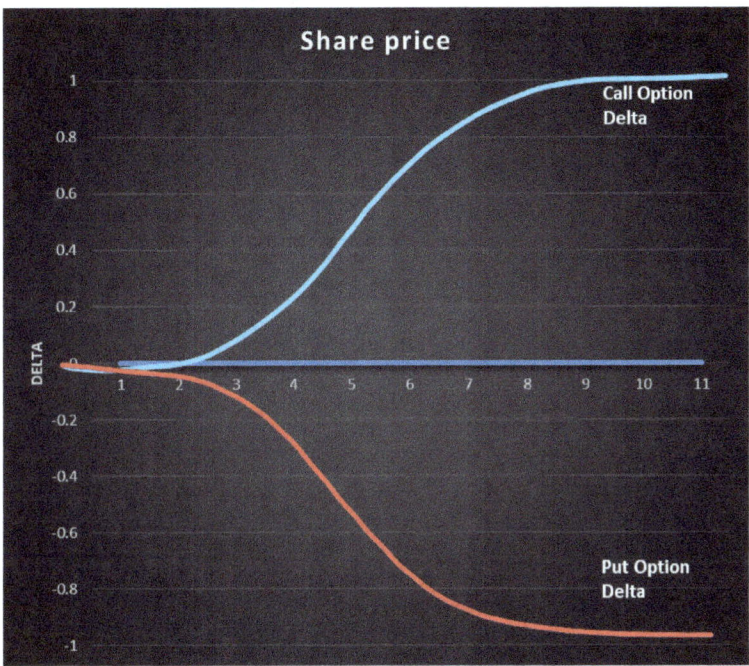

The PMCC strategy offers multiple trade-offs to "income-seeking" investors. If we do not have $165,000 necessary to purchase 100 shares of Amazon stock, we can simulate this position through PMCC's.

However, it is important to remember that we do not own Amazon stock in this strategy. We are merely simulating a long stock position. This difference is significant: When you buy a LEAP (call option that has twelve months or more to expiration) you are buying the right to every dollar above the strike price you selected for the duration of the LEAP. Your Amazon shares will never "expire worthless", your LEAP very well could. That's the trade-off.

A PMCC is simply the purchase of a call option that has more than a year till expiration and then selling a "front month" or the exact same call option you would have sold if you owned the stock.

| Covered Call | Poor Man's Covered Call |
|---|---|
| = Long stock + Short call option | = Long LEAPS option + Short call option |

PMCC formula:

*It's important to follow the following PMCC formula when initializing the PMCC trade.*

| PMCC Formula | | |
|---|---|---|
| LEAPS Price | < | Premium from short call sale + (Short call strike - Long call strike) |

## Setup:
- Buy an in-the-money (ITM) call option in a longer-term expiration cycle
- Sell an out-of-the-money (OTM) call option in a near-term expiration cycle

## Note:
The trade will be entered for a debit. It's important that the debit paid is no more than 75% of the width of the strikes. You need to make sure that the front month option you sell covers the time value of the long option you own.

## Example 1
Stock at $100
Purchase (Expiration #2) 90 call for $15
Sell (Expiration #1) 110 call for $5
Net debit = $10.00 on a 20-point-wide long call diagonal spread

Ideal Implied Volatility Environment: Low

Max Profit: The exact maximum profit potential cannot be calculated due to the differing expiration cycles used. However, the profit potential can be estimated with the following formula:

Width of call strikes - net debit paid + all premiums collected

How to Calculate Breakeven(s): The exact break-even cannot be calculated due to the differing expiration cycles used in the trade. As a rough estimate, the break-even area can be approximated with the following formula:

Long call strike price + net debit paid

## Example 2
Trade Date: January 18th 2019IYR Price: $77.73
Trade Details: Long Call at strike $68, expiring Jan-18-2021, at price $11.89
Sell Call at strike $80, expiring Mar-17-2020, at price $0.94
Total Premium Paid: $1,095
If we check back to our formula, this fits our criteria:
Difference between the 2 strikes + short call premium > LEAPS cost

## Advantages and Disadvantages
It's clear that the PMCC's income generating strategy can be very useful in replicating a covered call strategy if capital is a limiting factor. There is also another huge advantage to a PMCC strategy when compared to a traditional covered call strategy, assuming the stock rises over time you will see a considerably higher rate of return on the long LEAP (call) position than you would on the stock itself. The option is expected to have a delta close to 1 and nominally react to the underlying price changes in a similar manner, However, the option costs much less than the $165,000 initial outlay for 100 shares of Amazon stock assuming Amazon rises the return on your call option with be much higher (but the monthly income you generated will be the same in both strategies.

It is important for an investor to understand how to implement a successful covered call strategy, as well as, the factors that affect the pricing and volatility of an option that we have discussed in the prior chapters. When it comes to putting a PMCC position on you must follow the formula that is on the first page of the chapter. If you do not do the math you will run into obstacles at some point.

For example, you may need to adjust or unwind your PMCC position. This complication would incur relatively high trading costs as LEAPS usually trade with wider bid and ask spreads. In addition, if the price of the underlying changes significantly, the LEAP might behave irrationally and change in unexpected ways. This is where your emotion training will be tested as well as the homework you did on the stock you own the underlying LEAP on.

All of this reinforces the importance of the precise calculations that's required prior to putting the position on. After all, we would like to hold the LEAP for the duration and generate monthly income each month.

Finally, one still has the short call option from which premiums are collected and obligations might arise at expiration. So, this leg of the strategy needs to be monitored and adjusted if the need arises.

# CHAPTER NINE

## Vertical Spreads

Vertical spreads are created by taking position in multiple options of the same type (call or put) that have the same expiration but different strike prices. An investor would typically invest in vertical spread strategies when limited directional movement is expected or if they want to reduce their risk while still offering profit potential. If he or she has a strong expectation of a move in the underlying price but wants to limit their risk exposure, vertical spreads are a perfect strategy to employ. These spreads will provide protection if the investor is wrong about movement in the underlying price at a cost of capping the potential profit. We will explain this in more detail later.

First, let's take a closer look at two types of vertical spreads that are extremely popular among traders: bull and bear spreads. Bull spreads can involve either call or put options (bull call, bull put, bear call, bear put).

## BULL SPREADS

# Bull Call Spread

▸ Long Call ($X_1$=40, $C_1$=15) / Short Call ($X_2$=50, $C_2$=11)

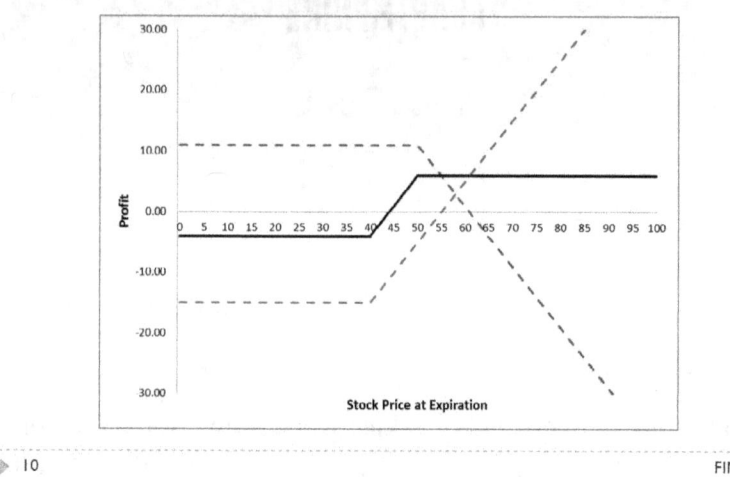

**Bull Call Spread**: A Bull Call Spread I created by purchasing a call option with a lower strike price and selling a call option with a higher strike price

**Bull Put Spread**: A bull put spread is created by purchasing a put option with a lower strike price and selling a put option with a higher strike price.

You might realize both bull spreads involve purchasing the option with lower strike price and selling the option with higher strike price. In terms of the premium cost and gain, this has differing implications.

Recall that call options become more expensive with lower strike prices (as call options give the right to purchase at the strike price purchasing right at a lower price creates higher intrinsic value). As a result, buying a bull call spread is a net-negative cash flow (low premium gained - high premium paid).

In contrast, bull put spreads will <u>always</u> be credit-spreads (net credit to account equity), because we will always buy a lower strike put and selling a higher strike put to enter the bull put spread. (remember puts get more expensive with higher strike prices)

## Bull Put Spread

▸ Long Put ($X_1$=40, $P_1$=9) / Short Put ($X_2$=50, $P_2$=15)

▸ $\pi = [Max(0, X_1 - S_T) - P_1] - [Max(0, X_2 - S_T) - P_2]$

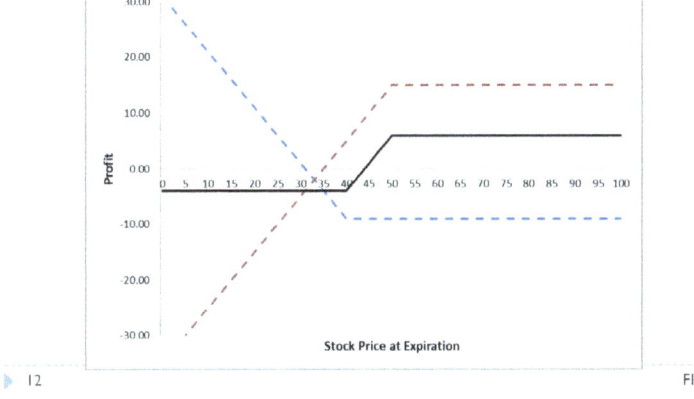

▸ 12                                         FIN 404

Both bull call spreads and bull put spreads will be profitable if the underlying price increases. There will be a cap on the profit, though, limiting the profit at a certain value no matter how much the underlying price increases. That's why it is rather suitable if the investor believes the rise potential is limited.

Since the maximum possible loss is also limited, bull spreads are not as risky as naked option investments or the most basic, standard, or simplest version of financial instruments, such as options, bonds, swaps, or futures.

| Maximum Profit and Loss | | |
|---|---|---|
| Vertical Spread: | Bull Call | Bull Put |
| Maximum Profit: | the spread between the strike prices minus the initial debit | Premium collected (credit) |
| Maximum Loss: | Premium paid (debit) | the spread between the strike prices minus the initial credit |

## BEAR SPREADS

A bear call spread is created by purchasing a call option with a higher strike price and selling a call option with a lower strike price. Bear call spreads can be a valuable investment strategy if the market insight is limited downside regarding the underlying price.

In this situation, a bear call spread will allow capped profits based on the falling underlying prices while providing limited loss profile in case the insight is wrong and the underlying price starts rising.

A bear put spread is created by purchasing a put option with a higher strike price and selling a put option with a lower strike price.
Both bear spreads involve purchasing the option with higher strike price and selling the option with lower strike price. In terms of premium cost and gain, this can have different implications (similar to what we saw in bull spreads).

Since call options get more expensive as the strike price goes lower (call options give the right to purchase at the strike price purchasing right at a lower price creates higher intrinsic value), bear call spreads will result in a positive cash flow (high premium gained - low premium paid).

Bear put spreads, however, will result in a negative cash flow since a put option with the lower strike price is going to cost less than put option with the higher strike price.

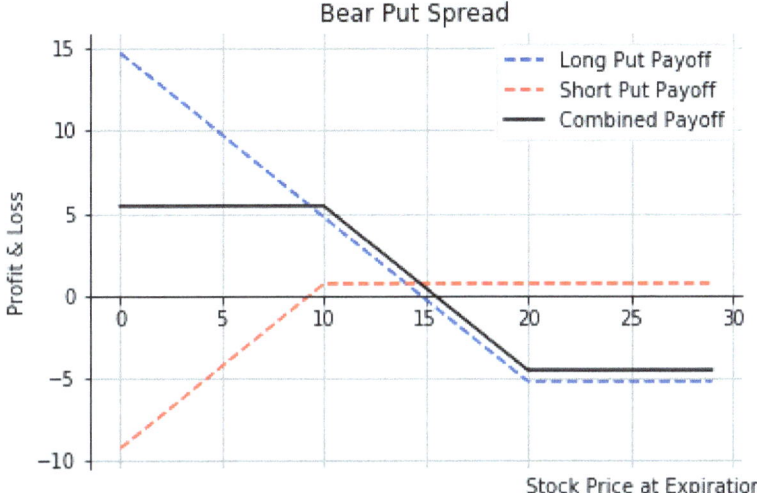

Both bear call spreads and bear put spreads will be profitable if the underlying price decreases.

There will be a cap on the profit, limiting the profit at a certain value no matter how much the underlying price decreases. That's why it is rather suitable if the investor believes the fall potential is limited.

Since the maximum possible loss is also limited, bear spreads are not as risky as naked option investments.

| Maximum Profit and Loss | | |
|---|---|---|
| Vertical Spread: | Bear Call | Bear Put |
| Maximum Profit: | Premium collected (credit) | The spread between the strike prices minus the initial debit |
| Maximum Loss: | The spread between the strike prices minus the initial credit | Premium paid (debit) |

Vertical spreads are one of the most convenient ways to bring in regular income from option investments while limiting the potential downside risk of a bad trade.

Another point about the usefulness of vertical spreads is that by adjusting the strike prices carefully you can design the exact spread you would like to achieve. If it's a bull spread, you can profit from increasing underlying prices, and if it's a bear spread, you can profit from decreasing underlying prices. But if your insight is wrong, your loss will have a maximum limit. Let's look at some examples that will make you have a much better understanding of 4 different vertical spreads that are commonly utilized by most experienced finance professionals.

**Example 1**: Bull call spread

| Bull Call Spread (@AMZN) | |
|---|---|
| Long call | Short call |
| Strike $1665, term: April 18, 2019 | Strike $1725, term: April 18, 2019 |
| Price: $140.00 | Price: $97.60 |

1/22/2019 Underlying AMZN trading at ~$1696

Long call: Strike: $1665, maturity: April 18, 2019 (trading at $140)
Short call: Strike: $1725, maturity: April 18, 2019 (trading at $97.60)
Net premium result: $140.00 - $97.60 = ($42.40) debit: net investment required

## Scenario 1:

April 18, 2019, Amazon share price increases to $1750.

The long call option is in-the-money, while the short call option (strike = 1725) is out-of-the-money:

Profit = Long Call position − Short Call position

Profit = [max(0, 1750 − 1665) − 140] − [max(0, 1750 − 1725) − 97.60]

The vertical spread would be worth $17.60 at expiration.

After adjusting with the initial investment, total net result is: $60 - $42.40 = $17.60 (Profit)

## Scenario 2:

Amazon share price decreases to $1550.

At expiration, the long call option would expire worthless, while the short call expires ITM

Profit = Long Call − Short Call

Profit = [0 - 140] − [max(0, 1550 − 1725) − 97.60]

Total result: ($ 42.40) loss

**Example 2**: Bull put spread

| Bull Put Spread (@AMZN) | |
|---|---|
| Long put | Short put |
| Strike $1645, term: April 18, 2019 | Strike $1785, term: April 18, 2019 |
| Price: $90.00 | Price: $149.25 |

1/22/2019 Underlying AMZN trading at ~$1696

Long put: Strike: $1645, maturity: April 18, 2019 (trading at $90)

Short put: Strike: $1785, maturity: April 18, 2019 (trading at $149.25)

$$\text{Spread} = (\max(0, 1645 - 1696) - 90) - (\max(0, 1785 - 1696) - 149.25) = (29.75)$$
$$\rightarrow \text{net credit}$$

## Scenario 1:

Amazon share price decreases to $1500. Both put options would be in-the-money in this scenario, but the short put option would be deeper in-the-money, as follows:

$1645 - $1500 = +145 (long put option position)

$1500 - $1785 = -(285) (short put option position)

Vertical Spread is now worth $145 - $285 = -$140

After adjusting for the initial premium, we received when we entered the position, the total net result is: -$140 + $59.25 = -$80.75 (Loss)

You can also see that this result is equal to strike price difference + premiums collected initially.

## Scenario 2:

Amazon share price increases to $1850.

The long-put option will expire worthless, while the short put option will expire ITM.

At expiration, we will collect the credit we received on the short put option minus the debit we paid for the long-put option.

**Total result**: $59.25 (Profit)

**Example 3**: Bear call spread

| Bear Call Spread (@AMZN) | |
| --- | --- |
| Long call | Short call |
| Strike $1800, term: April 18, 2019 | Strike $1600, term: April 18, 2019 |
| Price: $64.50 | Price: $167.00 |

1/22/2019 Underlying AMZN trading at ~$1696

Long call: Strike: $1800, maturity: April 18, 2019 (trading at $64.50)
Short call: Strike: $1600, maturity: April 18, 2019 (trading at $167.00)
Net premium result: $167 - $64.50 = $102.50 (credit: net premium collected)

**Scenario 1**:
Amazon share price increases to $1810.
Both call options would be in-the-money in this scenario, but the short call is deeper ITM:
$1810 - $1800 = $10 (long call option position)
$1810 - $1600 = $210 (short call option position)
Vertical Spread is now worth $10 - $210 = -$200

After adjusting with the initial investment, total net result is: $102.50 - $200 = -$97.50 (Loss)

Please note how loss is equal to difference between strike prices plus the initial net premium gain.

**Scenario 2**:
Amazon share price decreases to $1550.
Both call options would expire worthless and hence not be exercised

in this scenario, meaning the whole amount of initial investment would be lost.

**Total result**: -$42.40 (Loss)

**Example 4**: Bear put spread

| Bear Put Spread (@AMZN) | |
|---|---|
| Long put | Short put |
| Strike $1780, term: April 18, 2019 | Strike $1640, term: April 18, 2019 |
| Price: $135.30 | Price: $77.10 |

1/22/2019 Underlying AMZN trading at ~$1696

Long put: Strike: $1780, maturity: April 18, 2019 (trading at $135.30)
Short put: Strike: $1640, maturity: April 18, 2019 (trading at $77.10)
Net premium result: $77.10 - $135.30 = -$58.20 (debit: net investment required)

**Scenario 1**:
Amazon share price decreases to $1550.
Both put options would be in-the-money in this scenario, but the long put is deeper ITM:
$1780 - $1550 = $230 (long put option position)
$1780 - $1640 = $140 (short put option position)
Vertical Spread is now worth $230 - $140 = $90
After adjusting with the initial investment, total net result is: $90 - $58.20 = $31.80 (Profit)

**Scenario 2**:
Amazon share price increases to $1880.
Both put options would expire worthless and hence not be exercised in this scenario, meaning the whole amount of initial investment would be lost.

Total result: -$58.20 (Loss)

# CHAPTER TEN

## Iron Condors and How To Profit From Them

In the realm of all the varied methods that can be used to generate monthly income, few are as famous as the iron condor. Perhaps, it's just the visual that immediately arises in the brain when people here the phrase "iron condor." Everyone knows that the Condor is one of the largest flying birds in the entire world. The wandering Albatross is the only bird on the planet (alive!) that has a larger wingspan than the condor, whose wingspan runs from nine to ten-plus feet. The investment world uses this term to illustrate how a condor position should be put on and how it the overall strategy works to generate monthly income.

*What Is an Iron Condor?*

An iron condor is an option strategy that involves four different contracts. Some of the key features of the strategy include:

An iron condor spread is constructed by selling one call spread and one put spread (same expiration day) on the same underlying instrument.

All four options are typically out–of–the–money (although it is not a strict requirement).

The call spread and put spread are of equal width. Thus, if the strike prices of the two call options are 10 points apart, then the two puts should also be 10 points apart. Note that it doesn't matter how far apart the calls and puts are from each other.

Most often, the underlying asset is one of the broad-based market indices, such as SPX, NDX or RUT. But many investors choose to own iron condor positions on individual stocks or smaller indices.

When you sell the call and put spreads, you are buying the iron condor. The cash collected represents the maximum profit for the position.

It represents a 'market neutral' trade, meaning there is no inherent bullish or bearish bias.

Predominantly, because the iron condor has a potential for you to lose part or all of you money on the position regardless of what direction the S&P 500 moves, however your loss is limited to the margin required in order to put the trade on minus the premium you collected as monthly income. The goal of the strategy is to sell options that are far enough out-of-the-money that the S&P 500 never breaches one side of your spread.

**EXAMPLE 1**:

| Iron Condor Strategy (@SPY) | |
|---|---|
| Long put | Short put |
| Strike $245, term: April 18, 2019 | Strike $255, term: April 18, 2019 |
| Price: $3.00 | Price: $4.80 |
| Long call | Short call |
| Strike $285, term: April 18, 2019 | Strike $275, term: April 18, 2019 |
| Price: $1.25 | Price: $4.00 |

1/18/2019 Underlying SPY trading at ~$265

Long put: Strike: $245, maturity: April 18, 2019 (trading at $3.00)
Short put: Strike: $255, maturity: April 18, 2019 (trading at $4.80)
Short call: Strike: $275, maturity: April 18, 2019 (trading at $4.00)
Long call: Strike: $285, maturity: April 18, 2019 (trading at $1.25)

Premium from put and call sales: $4.80 + $4.00 = $8.80
Expense from put and call buys: $3.00 + $1.25 = $4.25
Net result from proceedings: $8.80 - $4.25 = $4.55
Also shows maximum potential profit and maximum loss of $5.45

Please note that the puts are structured with out-of-the-money strikes. The long put is deep out-of-the-money relative to the short put; thus, the short put position is more expensive and creates a profit margin over this range between the strike prices.

Similarly, you can see how calls have also out-of-the-money strikes with the short call having a strike price closer to ATM than the long call. The overall result is limited potential profit at an underlying price range.

## Scenario 1:

The SPY stays at or around $265 on the expiration date of April 18.

In this scenario, all the options they were both bought and sold expire worthless and $4.55 profit from the difference between long and short option premiums is realized (this $4.55 is realized and deposited into your investment account as soon as the position is placed and can be used as monthly income).

## Scenario 2:

SPY falls and stays below $245 on the expiration date of April 18.

In this scenario, the SPY broke through one of our wings and began eating away at our margin. The short put will cover the loss of $10 (margin) which is the difference in the two strike prices we selected ($255 - $245) since it is in-the-money on expiration.

When we subtract the premium, we collected of $4.55, this will give the net loss from the strategy: $10 - $4.55 = $5.45 (maximum possible loss)

### Scenario 3:

Underlying falls below $245 on the expiration date of April 18.

In this scenario, we can demonstrate why Scenario 2 created the maximum loss. At any value underlying price goes below $245, our long-put position will start to be in-the-money and offset the further losses that the short put will create. So, let's say underlying price falls all the way to $200, our short put will be in-the-money $55 ($255-$200) while our long put will also be in-the-money $45 ($245 - $200), offsetting the losses after $10 loss that occurs when long put option is at-the-money. So, loss is again $10 - $4.55 = $5.45

### Scenario 4:

Underlying rises to $275 on the expiration date of April 18.

In this scenario, all the options will again be out-of-the-money, resulting in $4.55 maximum profit once again.

### Scenario 5:

Underlying rises to $285 on the expiration date of April 18.

In this scenario, maximum loss will occur one more time, since only short call will be in-the-money with $10 ($285 - $275); and, when we subtract our profits from premium: $10 - $4.55 = $5.45.

### Scenario 6:

Underlying rises above $285 on the expiration date of April 18.

In this scenario, like Scenario 3, long call option will kick in and start to offset the losses from the short call position and maximum possible loss will remain the same at $5.45

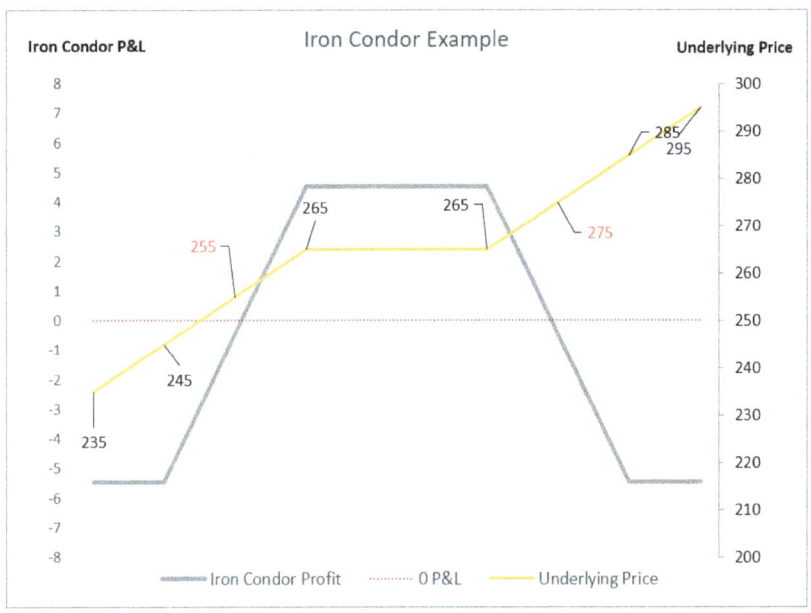

Here is a visualization of the iron condor example. Notice how strategy profits between $255 and $275 values of the underlying price? Also, you can see that below $245 and above $285, loss become a flat line, meaning maximum loss is reached.

You might have realized that although looking more complex than covered calls initially, iron condors have a more straightforward P&L profile that in the end makes comprehension and working with them easier than it is initially thought. Another reason for this phenomenon is because it is a combination of 2 spreads on both ends of the price movement, unlike the covered call that is a capped profit profile on one end and changing loss profile on the other (diverging to zero as the underlying price keeps falling).

*Asymmetric Iron Condors*
What if we designed it in a way that one of the spreads had different characteristics or boundaries? This is possible by adjusting the strike prices of either spread. Let's see an example where the call spread is looking different.

| Iron Condor Strategy (@SPY) | |
|---|---|
| Long put | Short put |
| Strike $245, term: April 18, 2019 | Strike $255, term: April 18, 2019 |
| Price: $3.00 | Price: $4.80 |
| Long call | Short call |
| Strike $290, term: April 18, 2019 | Strike $270, term: April 18, 2019 |
| Price: $0.65 | Price: $6.47 |

1/18/2019 Underlying SPY trading at ~$265

Long put: Strike: $245, maturity: April 18, 2019 (trading at $3.00)
Short put: Strike: $255, maturity: April 18, 2019 (trading at $4.80)
Short call: Strike: $270, maturity: April 18, 2019 (trading at $0.65)
Long call: Strike: $290, maturity: April 18, 2019 (trading at $6.47)

Premium from put and call sales: $4.80 + $6.47 = $11.27
Expense from put and call sales: $3.00 + $0.65 = $3.65
Net result from proceedings: $11.27 - $3.65 = $7.62 (Also shows maximum potential profit)

You may realize that potential maximum profit increased compared to the previous example. However, this will come with a cost. We will realize that potential maximum loss has also increased on the call spread side. So, the Scenario 1-2-3 remains unchanged where the underlying price falls or stays flat.

Let's look at when the underlying price increases in Scenarios 4-5-6.

**Scenario 1**:
Underlying stays at $265 on the expiration date of April 18.
In this scenario, all the options involved expire worthless and $7.62 profit from the difference between long and short option premiums is realized.

## Scenario 2:

Underlying falls to $245 on the expiration date of April 18.

In this scenario, all the options except the shorted put with $255 strike expire out-of-the-money. The short put will result in a loss of $10 ($255 - $245) since it is in-the-money on expiration.

When we subtract the premium profit of $4.55, this will give the net loss from the strategy:

$10 - $7.62 = $2.38

## Scenario 3:

Underlying falls below $245 on the expiration date of April 18.

In this scenario, we can demonstrate why Scenario 2 created the maximum loss. At any value underlying price goes below $245 our long-put position will start to be in-the-money and offset the further losses that the short put will create.

So, let's say underlying price falls all the way to $200, our short put will be in-the-money $55 ($255-$200) while our long put will also be in-the-money $45 ($245 - $200).

This offsets our losses after $10 loss that occurs when long put option is at-the-money. So, loss is again $10 - $7.62 = $2.38

## Scenario 4:

Underlying rises to $270 on the expiration date of April 18.

In this scenario, all the options will again be out-of-the-money, resulting in $7.62 maximum profit once again.

## Scenario 5:

Underlying rises to $290 on the expiration date of April 18.

In this scenario, maximum loss will occur one more time since only short call will be in-the-money with $20 ($290 - $270).

And, when we subtract our profits from premium differences $20 - $7.62 = $12.38.

**Scenario 6**:

Underlying rises above $290 on the expiration date of April 18.

In this scenario, like Scenario 3, long call option will kick in and start to offset the losses from the short call position and maximum possible loss will remain the same at $12.38.

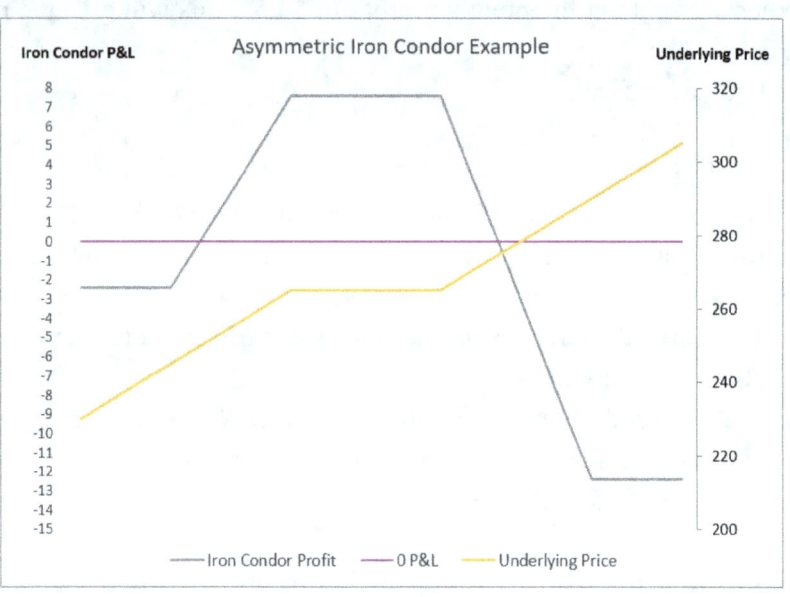

As you can see, by widening the spread between call options, we have created a higher maximum profit profile of $7.62. However, on the call option side (as underlying price increases), potential maximum loss also increased to -$12.38.

The power of creating such tailored strategies with options allows investors to invest in their insight much more precisely than conventional investment techniques. For instance, if you were to expect more downside than upside you could increase your profit by increasing the upside loss potential. Or, similarly, if you see more upside probability in the future compared to downside due to market conditions, cycles, fundamentals, timing, politics, or any other reason you might have, you could design the iron condor asymmetric in a way that the put spreads are larger than the call spreads.

# CHAPTER ELEVEN

## Risk Considerations

Options are risky investments not only because they create leverage, but also because they take expertise-level knowledge and/or experience to understand their behaviors. Once you understand the fundamentals of basic option strategies, it becomes much easier to understand and anticipate behaviors of structured derivative products.

In this chapter, we're going to look at some of the risks and potential losses that may result from investing in options.

Before we elaborate on that, it might be useful to revisit some of the different risk categories.

*Directional risk:* The risk that comes from underlying price changes in an upward, downward, or flat direction.

*Volatility risk:* The risks associated with changes in the underlying security's volatility.

*Liquidity risk:* The risk of not being able to buy or sell specific components of the strategy.

*Covered Call Risks & Losses*

Although covered call strategies cut down the risks tremendously compared to naked call or put strategies, they still have a certain level of risk. It will be beneficial to understand and be aware of these risks for anyone who is interested in covered call investments.

Directional risk in covered calls: Covered calls have a potentially large loss profile, despite having a capped upside. Technically, loss is theoretically limited to the difference between the underlying price and zero (minus premium collected). Since the goal of the strategy is to retain the underlying stock shares, you would normally pick a stock that had sound fundamentals, historical track record, proven operation health, sustainable revenue growth, etc. Popular blue-chip stocks, such as Apple and Amazon, are good examples.

It is a very rare event for blue-chip stocks to diminish or go bust in a day; even less-established stocks usually don't lose all their value in a very short period of time. However, we must list the theoretical risks involved so that you're aware of the potential downside to covered calls.

Volatility risk in covered calls: Consider the components of a covered call position: a short call option and a long position in the underlying security (100 shares). We know that option prices increase as the underlying volatility is raised, and option prices decrease with lower underlying volatility. Because we are short a call option in this strategy, if the underlying volatility increases during the life of the option, the call option price would rise (holding all else constant). And, if we wanted to cover our short call position (buying back the call), we would have to purchase it back at a higher price.

In a scenario where the volatility fell during the option's life, it creates an opportunity to cover the short call position early at a lower price. In addition, the option price would decrease due to the time decay as we approach the expiration date (holding all else constant).

Most liquid assets can be instantly bought and sold at a continuous market price. And, if the asset is illiquid, that means you might not be able to sell it easily when you become a seller. This might imply that you have to give significant discounts and/or wait for a long time before you match with a seller, depending on the degree of illiquidity.

With covered calls, liquidity risk is small as you are buying an underlying and selling a call option. However, if the call options have unusual contract terms or maturity dates, it might have a liquidity problem. Similarly, if the stock involved is a small cap asset or belongs to a foreign exchange, you may encounter liquidity problems. It is not very likely with a listed company that has options on it, but still do your homework regarding this aspect of your strategy.

| Covered Call Maximum Loss |
|---|
| Underlying Security losses - Short call premium |

## Covered Call Loss Scenario:

Let's make an example of Amazon stocks where the investor owns 100 AMZN and shorts a call option on the same asset as underlying. (Let's say AMZN is trading at $1720 and the option costs $60, with 30 days to expiration and strike price of $1750.) During the life of the option, you have to hold the stock because otherwise your position would be a naked call. On the expiration date, if the option expires worthless, you realize your premium gains, but let's look at the loss side. If the underlying price falls all the way to $1000 in a crisis scenario, you would have lost $1720 - $1000 = $720 minus premium collected = -$660

Although $660 is a big loss, it shows us that covered call is not much more risk averse than investing in stocks. This would actually be -66,000 because of the 100-share multiplier for the contract.

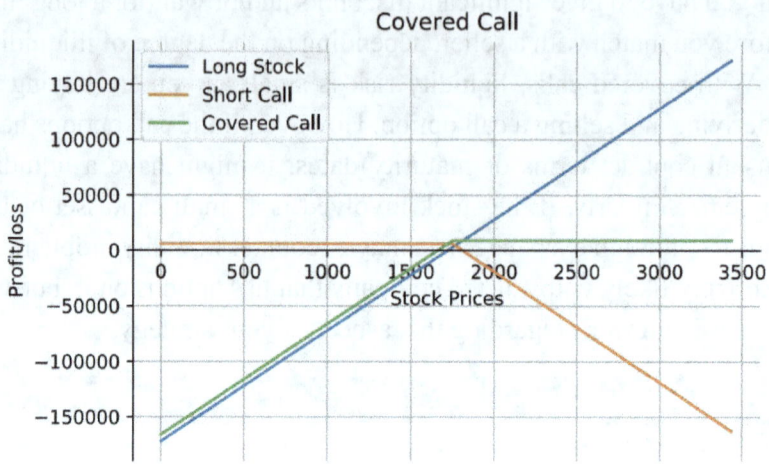

However, it also seems slightly less risky since you collect an option premium and these serve as a loss buffer in a bad scenario, making the losses smaller than they would normally be.

*Note: in an extreme scenario, such as the underlying stock price falling to zero, your maximum loss would be stock entry price minus premium collected, so a loss bottom-line slightly less than the full stock price (maximum loss scenario). Rare.*

Next, we'll discuss several option strategies that will provide more protection against potential maximum loss scenarios. (Excluding PMCC, which is a replication of covered call strategy, but with less capital)

## PMCC RISKS & LOSSES

PMCC has similar risk characteristics to covered calls. We will discuss the important differences of these strategies here. Most of these differences occur because of the LEAP component of the PMCC strategy. Let's look at those similarities and differences under relevant categories.

Directional risk in PMCCs: If the underlying price falls, PMCC will start losing value from its LEAP component. Since the LEAP component here will likely be cheaper than the actual underlying it-self, we can say that the nominal risk from the underlying price going down is lower compared to the covered call strategy. However, if you entered into a larger PMCC position, you might incur the same level of loss as your losses will be greater (in percentage terms).

Volatility risk in PMCCs: Volatility effects on a PMCC are more neutral since there is a long call and short call in the position, com-pared to only 1 option in the covered call. So, the volatility effects will be more-or-less offset in the PMCC. However, depending on the Vega Greek, there might still be some volatility exposure on the PMCC strategy.

Liquidity risk in PMCCs: Since the LEAP option replicates the long-stock component of a covered call strategy, it is a long term, deep in-the-money call option, with a very high delta. Sometimes, de-pending on the underlying and other features, such long-term options can be very illiquid. Illiquid assets such as these tend to have very high bid-ask spreads as well. It is important to keep liquidity in mind when evaluating such strategies.

| PMCC Maximum Loss |
| --- |
| Long call loss (LEAPS) - Short call premium |

## PMCC Loss Scenario:
Since the only difference between PMCC and a covered call is that PMCC uses deep in-the-money call options to decrease the capital intensity of the investment, the loss profiles are also very similar. But because the invested capital is less, potential losses are also less than they would be in a covered call scenario.

Let's say you invested in a PMCC structure where the long call op-tion (LEAPS) cost $200 and the short call option costs $50. As the underlying price falls, both call options will lose value. And, on the expiration date, if the underlying is below the strike of the short call option, it will expire worthless.

However, LEAPS will also lose some value. Technically, the maximum loss LEAPS can incur is its full price ($200) and loss will be that minus the premium collected. So, if the LEAPS is worth $150, the loss will be $200 - $150 -$50 = 0.

If the LEAPS' value goes all the way to 0, loss will be $200 – 0 - $50 = $150.

### Iron Condor Risks & Losses

Iron condors are a neutral strategy with a limited profit and limited loss profile. The strategy results in a loss if the underlying price is outside of the extreme strike prices (highest strike and lowest strike) of the 4 option contracts. These are usually regarded as a less risky strategy than covered call or PMCC.

Directional risk in iron condors: Although capped, there is a risk of losing money if the underlying price moves outside the far strike prices on either side of the strategy.

Volatility risk in iron condors: Similar to the PMCC, most of the volatility effects are expected to be offset since iron condor strategy involves 4 options positions that offset each other. Also, since the long and short options positions have very similar characteristics, the offset is going to be higher than the PMCC strategy (because the LEAP option has very different Greeks compared to the short call option).

Liquidity risk in iron condors: Like the other strategies we've discussed, general liquidity dynamics apply to the iron condor strategy as well.

### Vertical spread risks & losses

Vertical spreads resemble both covered calls and iron condors in different perspectives and they are very risk-averse products if the investor knows what he/she is doing.

Directional risk in vertical spreads: Vertical spreads are risk-averse due to the capped profit and capped loss on either side of the payoff profile. If your insight is directionally wrong, there is a limited loss potential with the vertical spread. However, if you enter into a large position (for example, long 10 calls and short 10 calls), you may still incur significant losses if the trade moves against you.

Volatility risk in vertical spreads: Similar to iron condor and PMCC strategies, the volatility effect is likely neutral due to the option positions' offsetting effect on the total Vega exposure.

Liquidity risk in vertical spreads: Option liquidity is an important aspect when creating a vertical spread strategy; it is important to avoid illiquid options in order to create the spread successfully.

| Vertical Spread Maximum Loss | |
|---|---|
| Bull Put / Bear Call: | High strike - low strike - net premium received |
| Bull Call / Bear Put: | Net premium paid |

Another important point to mention regarding option liquidity for vertical spreads is that the option time value continuously decreases over the life of this strategy. Over time, you may find your very popular option becoming much less liquid than before. That's why it's important to understand the dynamic nature of the options and they often may require a close eye on them before, during, and after you enter your investments. This might be one of the reasons why these potent and useful financial tools are usually at the hands of professionals.

**Capped Upside Potential**
Not all risks in the finance world are about losing your money. There are also risks of restricting profits. In many structured option strategies, if you see a scenario of a limited or reduced loss profile, this usually comes with the cost of capped profits. This usually means you are hedging your position by balancing the loss probabilities with sacrificing profit opportunities.

For instance, covered call and PMCC strategies are good examples of this phenomenon. When you are holding a stock that you favor for the long term, it might make sense to sell call options to make some extra profits on a flat market by collecting option premiums like a real investment professional. However, if a premature rally started for your underlying stock, you might lose all the potential upside since your short call position will cancel out the profits from the increase in the underlying price.

The above paragraph explains one of the reasons why structured option strategies require a mastery of market fundamentals as well as option fundamentals. A strategy like covered calls can be an amazing investment tool during flat markets. If you compare this ideal scenario with an investor who is only long in his/her favorite stock, the investor would be wasting his/her capital for years without profit from price gains.

Vertical spreads have similar trade-offs as the iron condor strategy except that one side of the spread is potential profit and the opposing side is potential loss. Recall that the iron condor's P&L profile is made possible by applying 2 spreads involving a total of 4 options, while vertical spreads only employ 2 total options equaling 1 spread.

If you have very strong predictions that the underlying security will move toward one side (up or down), vertical spreads can be the perfect strategy to use.

Regardless of the strategy you choose, if you understand and accept the benefits and the risks involved, you can maintain a clear mindset and will stay on top of your investing goals. There is a wealth of academic and professional material on behavioral finance and investment psychology that can help you to master this. Ultimately, your own experiences will be the key element in mastering powerful investment strategies and achieving success.

# CHAPTER TWELVE

## Successful Strategy Adjustments

Options are products with expiration dates and many of their characteristics change constantly, depending on many factors, including the passage of time. This dynamic nature of options requires investors to manage and adjust their investment strategies if necessary. This chapter focuses on popular methods used to adjust option positions.

### ROLLING COVERED CALLS

Rolling a covered call means covering the option component of your strategy by buying back the short call position and opening another short call position with a different strike and/or expiration date.

Let's imagine you have a covered call position in Amazon Inc. (AMZN). The underlying stock is currently worth $1622, and you are selling call options at a strike price of $1650 with 40 days left until expiration. Let's say you sold these options at $28.50 each and we'll make the assumption that you want to hold onto your shares in AMZN stock.

Hypothetically, if AMZN shares jump to $1700 close to the maturity date, chances are you will have to sell your long stock position. A very common practice to avoid losing the long position is to buy back the short call option and replace it with the more relevant option. The call options you sold will cost more than $28.50 due to the increase in the underlying price.

Let's say you are able to close the short call option position at around $55. Now you are at a loss of $55 - $28.50 = $26.50 (x 100 shares) = ($2,650).

You've also made $1700 - $1622 = $78 (x 100 shares) = $7,800 from the price increase of your 100 shares in AMZN stock. So, the cost to close the short call position is more than covered.

You can also roll your position "up and out". This means bumping up the strike price and rolling out the maturity date. A good example can be a $1780 call option with maturity of 60 days, for $42. Now your previous position is closed, and you can add this new profit from the option proceeds once they expire.

On the negative side, now you have to wait +60 days to be able to realize your profits and this increases the riskiness of your strategy.

Also, it might be tempting to continue rolling your position every time the underlying price increases unfavorably, but it is important to keep in mind that every adjustment realizes current losses for potential future profits. Not only does this increase the risk, this makes it more difficult to exit the trade profitably. Every time you roll the position, you incur costs that are realized. You must evaluate whether the potential future profit is worth realizing current losses.

In a different scenario, stock prices might start decreasing. After a threshold, this means your net position of covered calls will turn into loss. In this case, you might want to close your short call position by buying back the call options at a lower price and replace the short position by shorting call options with a lower strike price. This is known as "rolling down" the position – lowering the strike price closing the previous position and opening a new option position at a lower strike.

## ROLLING PMCCS

Rolling the short call option component is very similar to rolling a covered call strategy. However, PMCCs also have a long call option component (LEAPS) that is different from the covered call strategy. Although LEAPS are long-term products with +1-year maturity dates, this is still considered a short-to-mid timeframe for the traditional investor.

For instance, entering a PMCC investment by initially buying a 2-year LEAPS option and replacing it with a new 2-year LEAPS option after one year would be an example of rolling out.

Another situation could be when the underlying asset starts losing its value. In this case, your deep in-the-money LEAPS option will start losing its deep in-the-money feature. And, as a result, the delta will most likely decrease. This is not very desirable if you are trying to simulate a long stock position with delta as close to 1 as possible. By replacing (rolling down) your LEAP option with an option at a lower strike price, the position will be deep in-the-money again and the long position reacts as close to the underlying stock as possible. You will still have to do the adjustments for the short call as you would in a regular covered call investment.

## ROLLING IRON CONDORS

Rolling an iron condor is a slightly more complicated process than rolling covered calls or PMCCs. Let's consider the following example and evaluate potential adjustments for this strategy:

| Iron Condor Strategy (@SPY) | |
|---|---|
| Long put | Short put |
| Strike $245, term: April 18, 2019 | Strike $255, term: April 18, 2019 |
| Price: $3.00 | Price: $4.80 |
| Long call | Short call |
| Strike $285, term: April 18, 2019 | Strike $275, term: April 18, 2019 |
| Price: $1.25 | Price: $4.00 |

1/18/2019 Underlying SPY trading at ~$265

Long put: Strike: $245, maturity: April 18, 2019 (trading at $3.00)
Short put: Strike: $255, maturity: April 18, 2019 (trading at $4.80)
Short call: Strike: $275, maturity: April 18, 2019 (trading at $4.00)
Long call: Strike: $285, maturity: April 18, 2019 (trading at $1.25)

Premium from short put and short call: $4.80 + $4.00 = $8.80
Expense from long put and long call: $3.00 + $1.25 = $4.25
Net result from proceedings: $8.80 - $4.25 = $4.55 (Also shows maximum potential profit)

## STOCK MOVES UP: ROLLING UP THE PUT SPREAD

We already know that iron condor is constructed by combining 2 spreads: a call spread and a put spread. The put spread regulates the strategy's relation with the lower end of the underlying price while the call spread regulates the strategy's relation with the higher end of the underlying price.

Let's say the underlying asset is moving upward and nearing the farthest strike price ($285). In this case, the underlying price may move out of the strategy's profitable range and start incurring losses.

A potential adjustment could be rolling the lower leg (i.e. the put spread) by closing the current put spread and opening a new spread at higher striker prices.

Let's say underlying price increases to $270 from $265. By buying a $255 put option and selling a $265 put option we can create a new payoff profile for our investment.

This is shown visually in the next chart:

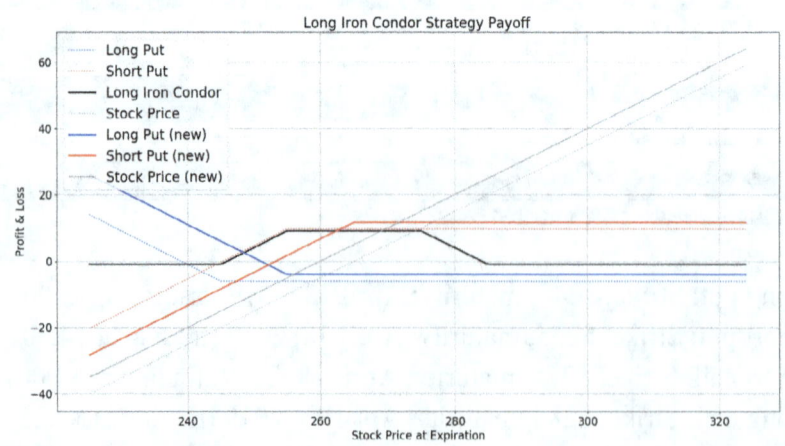

Profitable range shrinks: Initially, $275 - $255 = $20, now the profitable range is $275 - $265 = $10 only.

By increasing the strike of the put spread we're selling, we would create more of an option premium than we initially created. This means our total collected premium can be expected to be higher than $4.55 now. For demonstration purposes, let's say the new total premium collected is $6, so $1.45 premium was added to the initial number from increasing the strikes of the put spread.

The increase of premium collected means if the strategy works, our maximum potential profit will also be increased (from $4.55 to $6.00). However, the probability of success is decreased since we have narrowed the range of profitability (from $20 to $10).

Remember, maximum loss for iron condors is the strike price difference of spreads minus premium collected. So, for the put side, it would be ($265 - $255) - $6 = $4. As you can see, our maximum loss level is also improved from (($265 - $255) - $4.55 = $5.44) $5.44 to $4.00.

| Iron Condor Adjustment (Rolling up the put spread) | |
|---|---|
| Pros | Cons |
| Higher maximum profit | Narrower profitability range |
| Lower maximum loss | Increased commissions due to additional option trades |

## STOCK MOVES DOWN: ROLLING DOWN THE PUT SPREAD

Now, let's consider a scenario where the underlying stock price goes down. Similar to the "rolling up" adjustment we made for the put spread, we can roll down the call spread by closing the current call option positions and replacing them with call options at lower strike prices.

Let's say this creates an additional $0.95 option premium.

Possible option replacement operation:

Old Short Call: Strike: $275, maturity: April 18, 2019 (trading at $4.00)

Old Long Call: Strike: $285, maturity: April 18, 2019 (trading at $1.25)

Old Net Premium: 4 – 1.25 = $2.75

New Short Call: Strike: $270, maturity: April 18, 2019 (trading at $4.00)

New Long Call: Strike: $280, maturity: April 18, 2019 (trading at $1.25)

New Net Premium: 5.45 – 1.75 = $3.70 (extra $0.95)

Similar to the previous adjustment, now we have $4.55 + $0.95 = $5.50 option premium collected. This is also our new maximum profit level. Our maximum loss will also be improved, from (($280 - $270) - $5.5 = $4.50) $5.44 to $4.50.

Remember, we have to realize current losses every time we adjust our positions. This makes it less likely for the overall strategy to realize a profit when exiting the trade. An extremely popular strategy using iron condors is to put the trade on 60 days out and close it after the desired time decay profit.

# ROLLING VERTICAL SPREADS

Vertical spreads can be adjusted similar to the iron condor strategies. Let's analyze them under two categories.

1- Debit Spreads (bull call & bear put):

| Bull Call Spread (@AMZN) | |
| --- | --- |
| Long call | Short call |
| Strike $1665, term: April 18, 2019 | Strike $1725, term: April 18, 2019 |
| Price: $140.00 | Price: $97.60 |

1/22/2019 Underlying AMZN trading at ~$1700

Long Call: Strike: $1665, maturity: April 18, 2019 (trading at $140)
Short Call: Strike: $1725, maturity: April 18, 2019 (trading at $97.60)
Net Premium Result: $97.60 - $140 = -$42.40 (debit: net investment required)

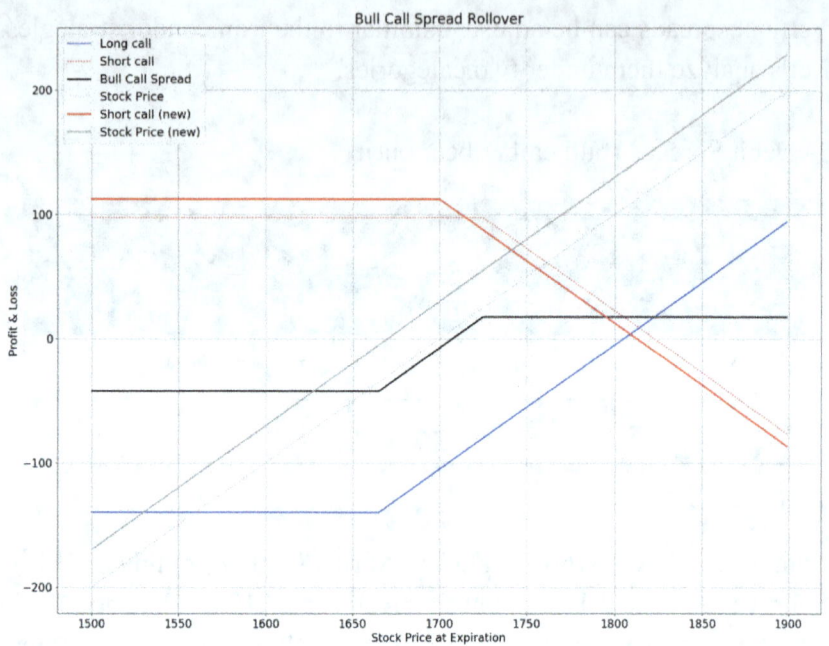

In the scenario above, we see the underlying stock going slightly down to $1670 from the initial price of $1700. In this case, a particular adjustment we can consider is closing the short call position and replacing it with a more valuable call option with a lower strike price. Let's say we short $1700 call option instead of $1725. For simplification, let's assume this creates an extra $15 premium by selling a more expensive call option.

Now our net debit is $27.40 instead of $42.40. This lower the upside chances a little, but if the stock price was to continue to fall, it also helps the position lose less money by decreasing the maximum possible loss. If the stock price falls beyond the long call's stock price of $1665, both options would have expired valueless and the maximum loss is the net debit paid, which is $27.40 instead of $24.40.

| Bull Call Adjustment (Rolling down) | |
|---|---|
| Main benefit | Main loss |
| Reduces maximum loss | Restricts maximum profit |
| | |

In a bearish debit spread adjustment, a.k.a. bear put spread adjustment, we would be on the wrong side if the underlying stock started increasing. Similarly, in this case, it might be beneficial to roll up the short put spread. As put options become more valuable as the strike price increases, this adjustment will allow to us to collect additional premiums and decrease the net debit position.

The benefits of the adjustment are very similar to the adjustment we made to the bull call, as follows:

| Bear Put Spread (@AMZN) | |
|---|---|
| Long put | Short put |
| Strike $1780, term: April 18, 2019 | Strike $1640, term: April 18, 2019 |
| Price: $135.30 | Price: $77.10 |

1/22/2019 Underlying AMZN trading at ~$1696

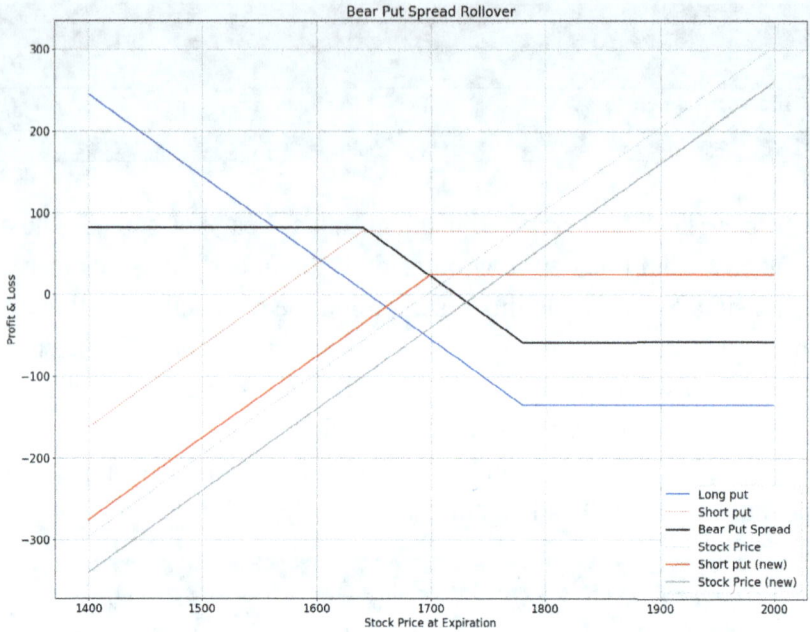

Short Put: Strike: $1640, maturity: April 18, 2019 (trading at $77.10
Long Put: Strike: $1780, maturity: April 18, 2019 (trading at $135.30)
Net Premium Result: $77.10 - $135.30 = -$58.20 (debit: net invest-
ment required)

## CREDIT SPREADS (BEAR CALL & BULL PUT)

As the name suggests, credit spreads provide a credit by collecting a
net option premium (more than you are paying on premium for your
long position). With a bear call spread, you're selling a call option at
a lower strike price than the call option you're buying. This provides
a net credit for the total position.

Similarly, bull put spreads also result in a net credit. This is because the strategy involves selling a more valuable put option (higher
strike) than the one you are buying (lower strike).

One common adjustment for credit spreads is to add another
spread to the position so that the overall strategy becomes an iron
condor. This is fairly intuitive; recall that iron condors are composed

of two vertical option spreads. Therefore, it makes sense that we can turn any vertical spread into an iron condor by adding a corresponding vertical spread in the opposite option type.

In our specific example using a bear call credit spread, we must sell a put credit spread having the same distance between strike prices as our original call spread.

If you look closely at the strike prices in the table below, the $10 difference between put strikes matches the $10 difference between call strikes. This is to provide the symmetric structure of an iron condor.

| Iron Condor Strategy (@SPY) | |
|---|---|
| Long put | Short put |
| Strike $245, term: April 18, 2019 | Strike $255, term: April 18, 2019 |
| Price: $3.00 | Price: $4.80 |
| Long call | Short call |
| Strike $285, term: April 18, 2019 | Strike $275, term: April 18, 2019 |
| Price: $1.25 | Price: $4.00 |

1/18/2019 Underlying SPY trading at ~$265

| Credit spread adjustment (iron condor transformation) | |
|---|---|
| Pros | Cons |
| Increases maximum profit | Narrows the profitable zone |
| Realignment around the current underlying price | Restricts profitability on both ends |

What are some of the benefits and disadvantages of this transformation?

The answer is simple: we increase the potential maximum profit of the position in exchange for a narrower profitable zone (i.e. probability of profit is lowered).

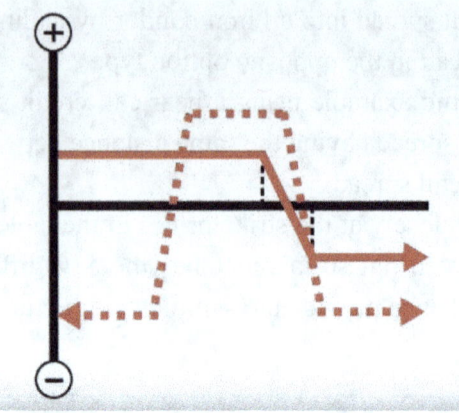

Bear Call Transformation VS Bull Put Transformation

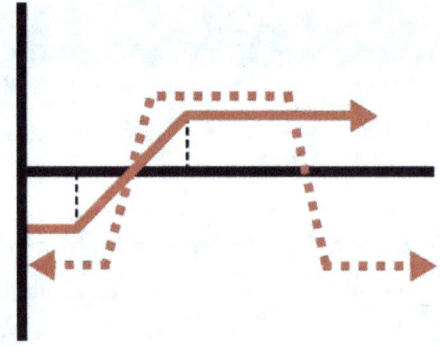

# CONCLUSION

Finally, rolling option positions can be a personal and subjective pursuit. Although there are common adjustments, such as the ones explained in this chapter, it still depends on your personal insight and expectations regarding how to navigate changing time and market conditions.

It's always better to start testing the waters when you're learning something new and gain expertise through smaller mistakes rather than devastating ones that might take a long time to recover and which will set you back. However, those are also usually the ones that contribute greatly to an investor's perception and discipline as well as help acquire seriousness and focus that's usually needed in the investment world.

## HERE IS A SUMMARY OF A FEW IMPORTANT ASPECTS OF OPTION ADJUSTMENTS:

*Adjustments are made to stay in the position, keep the position relevant or based on obligations.*

*Always count in your rolling costs, such as broker commission, fees, and spread width.*

*Rolling can be the much-needed blood for a position; but don't always expect a miracle. It usually means something is going wrong or didn't go as planned initially.*

*Always have a solid understanding of what you're doing and don't leave it to chance, with options and investment in general.*

# GLOSSARY

**Annualized**: Reflecting a rate based on an entire year.

**Bear Spread**: A mildly bearish option strategy.

**Bearish**: Expecting falling prices.

**Black & Scholes**: Merton Formula: A mathematical formula founded by Fischer Black and Myron Scholes to calculate option prices. Later contributed by Robert Merton to include dividend effect.

**Bull Spread**: A mildly bullish option strategy.

**Bullish**: Expecting rising prices.

*Call Option: A financial contract that gives the buyer the right, but not the obligation, to buy an agreed quantity of a particular underlying asset (i.e. financial instrument or commodity)*

**Call-Put Parity**: A check defining that a call and a put option with the same expiry date and strike price on the same underlying asset should have the same option prices. Under put-call parity, the option prices should match, yielding no profit or loss.

**Capital**: Wealth in forms of assets such as cash, cash equivalents, commodity or property owned by a person or business.

*Covered Call: A market neutral option strategy in which call option is sold and corresponding amount of underlying asset is bought covering the short call position hence the name covered call.*

**Crisis**: A sudden upset in the economy causing severe value loss for some or all of the financial assets. Also used as financial crisis or economic crisis.

**Delta**: An option Greek measuring how much an option's price is expected to change per $1 change in the price of the underlying asset.

**Derivative**: A derivative is a securitized contract between two or more parties whose value is dependent upon or derived from one or more underlying assets.

**Economic Growth**: Increase in the inflation adjusted value of goods and services. Usually calculated and published for quarterly and annualized periods.

**Expiry**: Used interchangeably with expiry date or maturity date. Used to define the date at which an option expires.

**Gamma**: Gamma is the rate of change in an option's delta per 1-point move in the underlying asset's price.

**Greek**: Option Greeks are values that measure how different factors affect an options price. Each option has its own unique greek values and they also change as other factors change and as time passes. Most common greeks are first order greeks named: delta, vega, theta and rho. Other first order greeks omega and epsilon as well as second and third order greeks are not as commonly utilized.

**Historical Volatility**: A statistical measure of volatility. Historical volatility is calculated by finding the standard deviation of returns for a financial security over a period of time.

*Implied Volatility: Implied volatility is a useful measure of volatility. Instead of looking at historical data (as in historical volatility) implied volatility extracts volatility from the market implication. It is calculated by reverse engineering the prices of options on the market. This calculation allows finding the average volatility that is being perceived as the right amount by other market players.*

**Index**: In finance, an index is a statistical measure of changes in a group of data points. It may represent a whole financial market where stocks are listed or other subcategories such as listed telecommunication or pharmaceutical stocks, 500 largest companies, growth stocks, emerging markets etc.

**Intrinsic Value**: An option's value is composed of two different kinds of values. One of them is its time value (in relation to the probabilistic opportunities based on time left to its maturity) and intrinsic value. Intrinsic value comes from the relation between option's strike price and the price of option's underlying asset. In short term it can be explained as options in-the-moneyness. If an option is in-the-money its intrinsic value is the difference between its strike price and underlying asset's price and if it's out-of-the-money option's intrinsic value is zero. Intrinsic value doesn't go below zero since options give the buyers the right but not the obligation to buy (if it's a call option) or sell (if it's a put option).

**Iron Condor**: An option strategy made with a call spread and a put spread with same maturity days but different strike prices.

**Junk Bond**: A bond with a high risk of not being paid back. Bonds are perceived as junk bonds usually when rating agencies rate them as below investment grade and high risk. Due to their risky nature junk bonds are also high yield bonds as they seek to attract investors, or nobody will invest in them with high risk and low yield.

**Leverage**: An investment technique used to achieve larger exposure with smaller amounts of capital. It can be used for leverage or increased exposure through financial vehicles such as borrowing money, borrowing assets, using derivatives etc.

**Long term investment**: An investment strategy involving buying and holding assets for a term longer than one year.

**Margin**: The difference between the value of a financial security that's being collateralized, and the loan amount borrowed against it from a broker to buy securities.

**Market**: Refers to financial marketplace where buyers and sellers trade financial securities.

**Maturity**: Maturity date, expiration or expiration date. The date when option's life expires. At maturity an option either expires in-the-money or out-of-the-money. In case it's out-of-the-money it will be valueless and worth zero dollars. If it expires in-the-money its value will usually be deposited to the owner's account after the settlement with the broker or financial institution.

**Maximum Loss**: Maximum amount of possible loss that can occur in particular strategies.

**Maximum Profit**: Maximum amount of possible profit that can be made in particular strategies.

**Mean**: The sum of the values of all observations or data points divided by the number of observations. A statistical average.

**Mutual Fund**: Basket of investments enabling investors to pool their money as a fund. Usually managed by a fund manager and a company that's operating the fund.

**Neuroeconomics**: A recent interdisciplinary field which attempts to link economics, psychology, and neuroscience.

**Normal Distribution**: A bell-shaped frequency distribution curve. Normal distribution is one of the most common continuous probability distributions.

*Options: Options are financial derivative products that give the buyer the right to buy (if it's a call option) or the right to sell (if it's a put option) an underlying asset at a pre-defined price (strike price) on a pre-defined date (maturity date).*

*Premiums: A premium is the total cost to buy an option, which gives the holder the right but not the obligation to buy or sell the underlying financial instrument at a specified strike price.*

*Put Option: A financial contract that gives the buyer the right, but not the obligation, to sell an agreed quantity of a particular underlying asset (i.e. financial instrument or commodity)*

*Quantitative Easing: An expansionary monetary policy used by central banks to inject money in order to increase economic activity. Most recently we have observed quantitative easing after the global 2008 crisis where Federal Reserve purchased massive amounts of government bonds from the market throughout the years which resulted in excessive cash entry to the markets creating low interest yields and increased economic activity. During such times investors don't have many incentives to keep their money in bonds. Since interest yields and cost of borrowing are extremely low all the extra money goes to fields that increase economic activity such as businesses, real estate investments, venture capital etc.*

**Recession**: A period of time when a country's economy experiences a slowdown, and this results in a contraction of business and economic activity as well as other socio-economic problems. When an economic recession happens to a big economy this can also trigger a global recession and cause many other countries to suffer similar consequences and disruption of healthy business cycle.

**Return**: Or financial return. In simply turns it defines the money made or lost in an investment. It can also be used with another word describing the time period the return refers to such as daily return, yearly return, quarterly return, monthly return etc.

**Rho**: An option Greek related to interest rates. It measures an option's sensitivity to the change in interest rates and if an option's rho is 1 that means an increase of 1% in interest rates will cause an increase of 1% in option's value.

***Risk: Financial risk is the probability of losing an investment partly or as a whole. There can be many different types of risk that should be calculated and evaluated before an investment such as: economic risk, liquidity risk, currency risk, management risk, default risk etc.***

**Risk Capital**: Risk capital is often referred to as "funds that are invested in high-risk, high-reward investments." To paraphrase this, it's money that you are willing to lose in order to achieve a higher gain. This is the money that speculative traders like to try and use to make those ten-bagger and multi-bagger wins. However, it's important to remember that when you lose money on puts and calls, you've lost not only the actual funds, but the time you've spent seeking out the speculative, higher-risk trades. As such, it's said (according to Business Dictionary) that risk capital which takes the full brunt of the effects of failures, misjudgments, uncertainties, and adverse circumstances."

**Risk-Return Profile**: Ideally an investment's risk should be aligned with the return it's offering. Risk-return profile is a very important phenomenon in finance and investors and analysts work very hard to seek out and identify investments with high return and relatively low risk.

**Risk-free**: Risk-free interest rate. A concept representing the theoretical rate of return of a zero-risk investment. Usually benchmarked with the United States government treasury bonds.

***Rolling Position: A common adjustment method in option investing/trading. Moving a position by replacing the options in portfolio with new options with different strike prices and/or expiry dates.***

**Safe Haven**: A place where you are protected from harm or danger. It can also mean an investment that keeps its value especially when others are falling in price.

**Share**: Share in the ownership of a company. Interchangeable with stock or equity.

**Short Selling**: The sale of a security that is not owned or that is borrowed by the seller. Short selling enables the investor to profit from a declining market or asset.

**Standard Deviation**: The standard deviation is a statistic that measures the dispersion of a dataset relative to its mean. It can be calculated after finding the variance as standard deviation is the square root of the variance.

**Stock**: Stock represents fractional ownership in a company. Can be used interchangeably with share or equity sometimes.

**Stock Market**: Stock markets are exchanges that allow, under certain regulated guidelines, the initial presentation of stocks to the public (an IPO) of a company, and the continued purchase and sell of the stocks on a daily basis. The most famous stock markets in the United States are the New York Stock Exchange, the Nasdaq, and the Chicago Stock Exchange.

**Strike Price**: The price (of underlying asset) at which a derivative contract can be exercised.

**Ten-Bagger**: Stock traders love ten-baggers because it means their initial investment or cost to purchase the stock contract is being returned at least ten times. This is a rare occurrence in the stock market.

***Theta: An option Greek related to time value of an option.***

**Time Decay: A measure of the rate of decline in the value of an option due to the passage of time. Used interchangeably with time value.**

**Time Value: The part of an option's value resulting from its time left to maturity. For example, an option with a current price of $1 and a theta of -0.10 will experience a time value loss of $0.10 per day.**

**Trading**: Action of buying and selling financial instruments.

**Underlying**: An asset used as an underlying to create derivatives based on.

**Valueless**: Carrying no value. For options, valueless means no intrinsic value nor time value.

**Variance**: A measure of volatility. The square root of variance is the standard deviation. it measures how much a price (or any value) is expected to deviate from its mean and can be calculated by a formula.

**Vega**: An option Greek related to volatility. It measures how much the price of an option would increase when volatility increases by 1%.

**Vertical Spread**: An option trading strategy. A vertical spread involves buying and selling of multiple options of the same underlying security, same expiration date, but different strike prices.

**Volatile**: An asset showing high price volatility.

**Volatility**: Relative rate at which, the price of a security changes. It can be a somewhat subjective concept and there are multiple ways to calculate volatility such as: historical volatility, implied volatility, stochastic volatility etc.

# ACRONYMS

**ATM**: At-the-money. An option is at-the-money when its underlying price is equal to its strike price.

**ETF**: An exchange-traded fund is an investment fund traded on stock exchanges and it allows investors to own a portfolio of stocks, bonds, commodities or other investment products for much lower fees than mutual funds.

**FED**: Abbreviation for the Federal Reserve System. Central Banking System of the United States which regulates the U.S. monetary and financial system since December 23, 1913.

**GDP**: Total value of all goods and services created by all the people and business entities in a country. Usually used interchangeably with economic growth.

**ITM**: In-the-money. A term used to describe that the option has intrinsic value. An option is in-the-money if the strike price is below the underlying asset's price for a call option and if the strike price is above the underlying asset's price for a put option.

**LEAPS**: Short for Long-Term Equity Anticipation Securities. LEAPS are options with long term expiry dates (typically more than 1 year and). They are expected to mimic the price changes of underlying security closely.

**Nasdaq**: "Nasdaq" was initially an acronym for the National Association of Securities Dealers Automated Quotations. It was founded in 1971 by the National Association of Securities Dealers (NASD), which divested itself of Nasdaq in a series of sales in 2000 and 2001.

**NPV**: Net present value. Present value of an investment determined by discounting all the future cash flows (positive and negative) at an appropriate rate.

**NYSE**: New York Stock Exchange. NYSE is a stock exchange located in New York City that is considered the largest equities-based exchange in the world, based on the total market capitalization of its listed securities.

**OTM**: Out-of-the-money. An option without intrinsic value. If this situation doesn't change and option expires out-of-the-money, it's value will be zero since time value will also be zero at expiry.

**PMCC**: Poor Man's Covered Call. A strategy created to replicate covered call strategy. This replication is achieved by replacing the long underlying asset position with long LEAPS options.

**QQQ**: An ETF which tracks NASDAQ-100 Index. While indices represent symbolic values calculated based on the values of assets that are included in them, ETFs are actual tradable financial instruments. In this case QQQ is the ticker name of an ETF which tracks NASDAQ-100 Index.

**Russell 3000**: A market-capitalization-weighted equity index tracking 3,000 largest U.S. traded stocks.

**S&P 500**: The Standard & Poor's 500. A stock market index based on the market capitalization of 500 large companies listed on the NYSE and NASDAQ.

**SPX**: A common symbol for the S&P 500 index.

**SPY**: Interchangeably SPDR or SPIDER. An exchange-traded fund (ETF) that tracks the Standard & Poor's 500 index (S&P 500).

**VIX**: Volatility Index. The CBOE Volatility Index, known by its ticker symbol VIX. It measures stock market's expectation of volatility implied by S&P 500 index options.

# ABOUT THE AUTHOR

David J. Melilli, AIF, is the Founder and President of Capstone Financial. David's mission as a fiduciary is to provide comprehensive investment advice while remaining objective, independent and completely client focused.

David began his financial services career in 2006 after earning his Series 7, 66, 31 and Accredited Investment Fiduciary designations. After obtaining the Accredited Investment Fiduciary (AIF) designation he decided to launch his own Fee-Based Investment Advisory Firm - Capstone Financial.

With increasingly complex financial markets and longer life expectancies, working with an investment professional is more important than ever. Our step-by-step income generating process helps us create an investment strategy that responds to our clients specific income needs and goals.

Providing quality investment advice is the cornerstone of our process and is paramount to the success of the client. We strongly believe that offering guidance increases the confidence and success of each client in reaching their income goals.

It's been more than a decade since founding Capstone Financial and David's passion for helping clients become financially secure and confident is as strong as ever.

www.ingramcontent.com/pod-product-compliance
Lightning Source LLC
Chambersburg PA
CBHW070350220526
45467CB00001B/322